DESIGNING THE WORLD'S BEST **RETAIL CENTERS**

DESIGNING THE WORLD'S BEST

ALTOON + PORTER ARCHITECTS

RETAIL CENTERS

images
Publishing

Published in Australia in 2004 by

The Images Publishing Group Pty Ltd

ABN 89 059 734 431

6 Bastow Place, Mulgrave, Victoria, 3170, Australia

Telephone: +61 3 9561 5544 Facsimile: +61 3 9561 4860

Email: books@images.com.au

Website: www.imagespublishinggroup.com

National Library of Australia

Cataloguing-in-Publication entry:

Designing the world's best retail centers: Altoon + Porter Architects.

ISBN 1 876907 45 2.

1. Altoon + Porter Architects. 2. Shopping centers. 3. Shopping malls.

725.21

Designed by The Graphic Image Studio Pty Ltd, Mulgrave, Australia

www.tgis.com.au

Film by Mission Productions Limited

Printed by Sing Cheong Printing Co. Ltd. Hong Kong

Contents

A Brief History of Retail Form

Across history, the development of culture is inextricably linked to the development of trade. From merchants on the spice and silk routes to teenagers at the mall, our very human desire for community and our instinct for commerce have led to the creation of gathering places with distinctive character, structure and use. From the beginning, retail forms were inspired by issues of context—the natural environment, the geographic situation, as well as their particular social, cultural, economic and political realities. Environments evolved as a response to particular needs and desires yielding unique formal expressions that reveal the diverse nature of retail itself.

A brief survey of the history of these markets informs our understanding of today's retail centers and suggests the shape of future prototypes. More than simply a lexicon, these precedents provide the DNA for the global, polymorphous, multicultural experience that is retail and remind us of the power of specificity in the creation of new shopping experiences in the now global village.

Agora

Perhaps the earliest formal structure to house markets was the Agora, the large open square northwest of the Acropolis in Athens. The civic and commercial center of the classical city, the Agora was reserved for public functions including meetings, theatrical events, festivals, markets, and elections. Excavations have revealed that in addition to the administrative buildings that surrounded the square, there were a number of other structures that were not built to serve a single public function but to provide shelter such as a fountain house that provided water for the crowds that frequented the Agora. The name agora came to describe the commercial centers of cities throughout Greece.

Caravanserai

Throughout Asia Minor, from the 8th to the 17th century, caravanserai were established to accommodate merchants, their animals and their wares. Built along the trade routes, usually spaced a day's journey apart, the caravanserai provided shelter and storerooms as well as hospitality and safety. Within the secure walls of the large rectangular building, travelers discovered food and a place to sleep. Just as importantly, they also found the companionship of others and valuable information about the road ahead. The bartering did not stop with the relay of news; the caravanserai, especially those in the cities, functioned as depots for goods and places for commercial transactions, to the point where they were often named after the special products traded within.

Forum

Forum is the Latin word meaning open space or market place. In ancient Rome, there were several forums, forming the administrative and corporate heart of the city. The architect Vitruvius designed the most famous, the Roman Forum, insisting on a proportion of 3:2 in length to width. For centuries, the Roman Forum served as the backdrop of political and cultural life. The location of many of the city's most important public buildings, the Forum was also the central venue for the exchanges of ideas at the rostra or public speaking platforms and for merchandise in the shops. The Emperor Trajan built the largest forum that covered an area of 25 acres and featured a market with three stories of shops and stores.

Bazaar

The word Bazaar, now familiar in numerous languages, is derived from the Farsi, reflecting the roots of these markets in the days of Islamic hegemony. With an architecture that combines both religion and commerce, the bazaar is one of the great achievements of Islamic civilization. The bazaars often had their beginnings in the caravanserai buildings where gradually agglomerated passages and arcades filled with merchants, docks, and houses under a domed enclosure.

As the network of buildings expanded, they came to include mosques, schools and bathhouses. Many of them have beautifully decorated façades and voluminous dome-like ceilings. Today's bazaars continue to preserve the form even as certain merchants disappear and are replaced, reflecting changes in society and commerce.

Souk

Souks are the street markets of the Middle East. Boutiques, flea markets, supermarkets and sideshows all in one place, they are central to the commercial life of cities across the Islamic world. All kinds of people shop at the souks for everything from foodstuffs to gold and jewelry. Collections of stands built up over the years take on a sense of permanence in spite of the cloth-covered aisles and the proliferation of vendors who spill out on to surrounding streets. Bargaining, a traditional custom, is expected.

Mercado

Mercados in Mexico and throughout Latin America combine elements of open-air street markets, and the more formal structures that house the bigger vendors in major cities. Many of the mercados have the qualities of Mexico City's Tianguis, street markets selling a variety of goods from produce to small appliances, clothing and handicrafts that set up in different neighborhoods each day of the week, providing variety and stability at the same time. The vendors' stalls are of metal tubing that can be quickly assembled and disassembled for transport. More spontaneous vending happens on the outskirts of the central marketplaces where local farmers, or more often their womenfolk, bring whatever is in season and present it on a basket or cloth on a street side.

Floating Market

The floating markets of Southeast Asia reveal the way that cultures adapt the market concept to suit their society and their geography. Small wooden boats laden with fruit, flowers, vegetables and other produce from nearby orchards and communities make a colorful and bustling scene at market time. Sellers come to meet and barter their products with other traders. The floating markets

are still important commercial centers for those living along the banks of rivers and canals without access to good roads. Large floating markets are not complete without their floating restaurants, floating gas stations and an occasional boat filled with tourists. Today, modern supermarkets and department stores have largely replaced the traditional floating markets, but a number survive and offer a bustling view of local commerce.

Haymarket

Haymarkets, where merchants sell their fruits, vegetables, meats, cheeses, and fish at extraordinary bargains, carry on the tradition of hawking wares that the Europeans first encountered in Northern Africa. The atmosphere is reminiscent of an earlier era when shoppers wandered freely among the stalls, enjoying smells and sounds impossible to find in antiseptic supermarkets today. As well as being a popular destination for cheap fruits and vegetables for local residents,

the haymarket has become a tourist destination in many locales.

Flea Market

The *marche aux puces* in Paris may be the most famous, but there are thousands of them all over the world today. America alone has approximately 500 flea markets, swap meets, open-air markets, farmers markets, antiques and collectibles markets, and special events with an estimate of more than one million vendors and one hundred million annual shoppers. Early flea markets dealt primarily in second-hand goods, including the upholstered furniture that attracted the notorious bugs. Today, flea

markets are any facility that rents a space to anyone that that has goods to sell to the general public. They offer anyone an unusual opportunity to start a retail business with little capital. Buyers love the spontaneity and the variety of treasure and junk that can be found on any weekend at the flea market.

Market Hall

True descendants of the Greek Agora and the Islamic Bazaar, the covered markets of European cities and a select few American examples are vibrant centers of commercial activity, especially for foodstuffs. Unlike the ubiquitous, but temporary, farmers markets in

town squares, plazas and even parking lots, the market halls boast a distinctive architecture often featuring metal canopies, long interior halls and arcades that presage the later development of the department store and the shopping center. Market halls have enjoyed a revival in US cities, including Los Angeles' Grand Central Market, Philadelphia's Reading Terminal Market, Seattle's Pike Place Market, and Little Rock's new River Market. Local governments and the developer community recognized the powerful draw of the market experience and renovated existing halls or built new ones as part of urban revitalization programs.

Galleria

The famed Galleria Vittorio Emanuele in Milan has been the model for numerous other shopping galleria but few compare to the original. The sumptuous covered arcade adjacent to the Duomo has been the traditional meeting-place for an informal business discussion, socializing, or just watching the people go by ever since it was built in the mid-19th century. At that time, the use of iron and glass for the roof was innovative, as was the concept of a covered arcade with shops on the ground floor, and offices and apartments on upper floors. Soon, it

would be copied in Naples, Moscow and other cities. Heroic in scale, the Galleria is also a key piece to the successful urban design at the heart of Milan. Designed in harmony with the rectangular architecture of Piazza Duomo itself, the entrance to the Galleria is incorporated into the neoclassical north and south sides of the square while the passage connects the cathedral in the piazza to the opera.

Piazza

While not strictly retail spaces, the great piazzas of Italy are formal precursors to the central courts of today's shopping centers. The Piazza Novana in Rome, the Piazza Del Campo in Siena, the Piazza San Marco in Venice, and others have inspired countless town plazas with their elegant open spaces and gracious fountains. However, it is the social space created by the piazza that captures the retail imagination. Cafés line the enclosures, providing refreshment and ringside seats for the ongoing show. More formal dining and shops are steps away under the arcades of the surrounding buildings. Promenading couples cross paths with businessmen, students and tourists enliven the urban fabric and step up the pulse rate for commerce.

Passages

Less imposing than the Galleria in Milan, shopping passages possess many of the same formal qualities. In cities throughout Europe, shoppers seek out select merchandise offered in the boutiques and shops in the covered arcades. The convenient passages offer protection from inclement weather, short cuts between streets and a sense of intimacy impossible to find on the broad boulevards. US examples include the Milwaukee Plankington Arcade and the Cleveland Arcade.

G.U.M.

The ornate Neo-Russian façade of G.U.M. (The Gosudarstvenny University Magazin), Moscow's State Department Store, takes up almost the entire eastern side of Red Square. Completed in 1893, the building features an intriguing combination of elements of Russian medieval ecclesiastical architecture and an elegant steel framework and glass roof, reminiscent of the great turn-of-the-century train stations of Paris and London. The three-story arcade, the largest collection of shops in Moscow, boasts a classic turn-of-the-century interior, comprising three parallel arcades centered on a fountain and overlooked by galleries. Light floods in through the building's glass roof, bringing a glow to souvenir stands, foreign stores and designer boutiques that fill the arcades. During the Soviet reign, there was a marked contrast between the ornate design of the building and its conspicuous lack of goods. Today the architecture is a perfect fit for stylish cafés and shops selling luxury goods.

Main Street

The nostalgic Main Street ranks with motherhood and apple pie as a quintessential part of the American dream. Generations knew it as the focus of community activity—civic and social as well as commercial. The elements repeated themselves in variations on streets across the country. Shops and offices, the bank, coffee shops and restaurants, the movie theater and a hotel lined the sides of the main thoroughfare, often joining with secondary streets at a town square dominated by the courthouse. Shopkeepers were individual entrepreneurs, not chains, and the best way to take advantage of the synergy of opportunities was on foot. Over the last 30 years, Main Street declined as demographics and social change led to the dominance of the suburban mall. Today, Main Street is enjoying a renaissance. The ease of access, the character of the architecture, the sense of place and the reassurance of community life are once again an important part of American neighborhoods.

Commercial Streets

World capitals have their version of Main Street, albeit in far more glamorous costumes. The long list—from Fifth Avenue in New York to Michigan Avenue in Chicago, from Wilshire Boulevard in Beverly Hills to Hollywood Road in Hong Kong, from the Champs Elysée in Paris to the Via Condotti in Rome to the Ginza in Tokyo—conjures up images of luxury and elegance. The broad avenues are home to the world's most exclusive merchants, including couture houses, furriers, fine jewelers and accessory shops of distinction. While many of these same merchants now have outlets in the finer malls, it is their presence on the famed shopping streets that creates their cachet. In recent years, the price points have dropped on some of the goods available, but the international appeal of these grand avenues has endured.

The Evolution of the American Shopping Center, 1960–2003

Origins

The origins of the American shopping center can be found in the genetic essence of America itself—on Main Street. Throughout the 19th century and up until the mid-20th century, customers found everything they needed on Main Street, where shops sat side-by-side with the all the rest of the social, political, cultural, religious, and recreational aspects of their lives. However, with the end of World War II, returning GIs saw the answer to their American dream in the affordable new residential developments in the suburbs. The lively urban mix of uses lining Main Street gave way to the regional shopping center where shopping was the singular attraction. The form has evolved over the decades in six distinct generations.

Generation I: The 'Doggie Bone' (1960s)

The first manifestation of this building type was characterized by a linear, open-air project, anchored at each end by a department store, with the mall itself tenanted with a varied mix of merchants. Often the center was constructed chronologically, as leases were consummated, resulting in an irregular structural grid that corresponded to the merchandizing strategies of each sequential tenant. Predominantly single-level structures, the malls were enclosed where an adverse climate influenced the design.

Generation II: The 'Wiggle Worm' (1970s)

The convenience of the suburban mall proved no substitute to the richness of the city experience and customers were quickly bored with the Generation I prototype. Designers, enamored by European shopping streets, reshaped the common area layout in a meandering manner that was influenced more by the shape of the site and ideal parking lot design than by the ordering mechanisms that are fundamental to architecture. Wide, second-floor platforms enabled easy movement side-to-side but created oppressive ground floor retail space below. More like constructed organic planning diagrams than thoughtful architecture, these projects were frequently dark by day and poorly lit at night, amorphous in plan and joyless at all times.

Generation III: The 'Galleria' (1980s)

The next iteration, birthed by architects rooted in the design traditions of Western civilization, introduced a language of forms and details that allowed them to create an 'Architecture of Retail' rather than a decorated box. These centers were characterized by strong repetitive structural systems, which defined the common area, reinforced by skylights above. The vertical circulation systems, customized handrails, bridges, and balconies, paving patterns, graphics and signage, lighting, and landscape systems were all designed to reinforce the concept. At last, the American shopping center began to approach the Gallerias and Passages of Europe in civic sensibility.

Generation IV: 'Entertainment Retail' (1990s)

The 'themed' retail–entertainment experience was intended to attract customers and sustain their interest through caricature architecture, surprise and storytelling. By employing style as a strategy over the substance of sound merchandizing, many of these ventures failed or simply did not meet expectations, and were re-merchandized at a lower price point before achieving success. The best examples of this typology result when the developer and architect produce a stage, the tenant becomes the playwright, and fashion itself is the entertainment.

Generation V: 'Precinct-Driven Retail' (mid-1990s, ongoing)

With the revitalization of downtowns occurring on a piece-by-piece, infill basis producing exceptional retail sales and high volumes of customers, the collective values of Main Street are enjoying a renaissance. The most recent prototype, the 'Precinct' center is characterized by multiple retail zones of like merchandise, a wide mix of experiences, and an authentic range of architectural expression. Here, the retail precincts are once again neighbors to office, hotel, residential, entertainment, dining, recreational, transit and civic uses. The total environment is scripted to meet a wide variety of lifestyle expectations. Values drive the joyful environment, just like a downtown.

Generation VI: 'Main Street' (2000s)

Main Street redux. However, this time it is being designed as a total environment from the ground up on greenfield sites rather than evolving over time. As a paradigm, it represents a system of values best understood in the original model of the 19th century that has been transformed to fulfill the lifestyle priorities of the 21st century. The new Main Street developments are characterized by a strong urban design framework, defined by streets with vehicular traffic and pedestrian-friendly zones, and building massing that mandates a minimum of two stories in height. A mix of uses supports this urban vision. Retail joins office, residential, hotel, restaurant, entertainment, dining, cultural, education, recreation, and civic use functions with the nexus of activity focused around the town square. An overlay of cultural, social, environmental and historic referents brings the development of the suburban retail shopping center full circle. Right back where it belongs.

Regional Malls

Regional Malls

Other species gather and store things, only humans shop for them. At times, we do so in remarkably similar fashion everywhere; at other times, we shop in stunningly different ways depending on our ethnic or national culture and customs. Global brands lead to homogeneity; local practices are infinite in their variety. Today, some people the world over usually dress in so-called Western or European clothes. Others favor traditional garments. We seek international brands in designer apparel, soft drinks, technology and motor vehicles, but for food prefer our regional or national cuisine and for entertainment our own music and dance. Whatever the case, an increasing percentage of all shopping is done in highly specialized structures of similar basic design— shopping centers, in which a number of independently owned businesses are made to function as if they were one.

The regional mall is among the most effective of these specialized retail structures. It delivers to the consumer greater choice among a wider range of products in a more convenient way than at any time in history. Initially an American innovation, the shopping center—and particularly the regional mall—has been adapted to local tastes in different parts of the world where shopping centers capture large and growing shares of the total retail market. From their beginnings in the 1960s in the United States, shopping centers have come to account for more than one half of all non-automotive sales, a figure that is now measured in the trillions of dollars.

In form, most regional shopping centers are streets turned more or less inside out. In style, inside they often seek to imitate the open-air marketplaces or retail streets of yesteryear. Like the bazaar or the town square on market day, they have become centers of community activity, conversation and entertainment as well as powerful engines of commerce. Their story is unparalleled in modern economic history.

John T. Riordan was Chief Executive of the International Council of Shopping Centers (ICSC) from 1986 to 2001 when he became ICSC Vice Chairman. At the same time, he was appointed Chairman of the Massachusetts Institute of Technology Center for Real Estate which grants a Master's Degree in Real Estate Development.

Al Mamlaka at Kingdom Centre

Riyadh, Kingdom of
Saudi Arabia

The design of the landmark Al Mamlaka complex, the three-story retail portion of Kingdom Centre, the Middle East's tallest building complex, reveals how culture shapes the retail experience. A traditional yet contemporary feel marks the first two levels, with the first level oriented toward leisure and youth and the second level oriented toward fashion and home. The top level—reserved for women only—responds to the unique needs of women in the local culture. This mall within a mall provides a private environment where women can shop and socialize in seclusion. The result is an intimate, relaxed setting—complete with spa, business center and food court—which favors the customer/merchant exchange. Private access ensures its exclusivity.

The entire retail complex is organized around a large central atrium filled with natural light streaming through continuous clerestory windows. Decorative screens made of perforated metal and sandblasted glass hang suspended from trusses and filter the sun's intensity. Transparent three-story kiosks vertically unify the design. Dramatic bridges connect the floors horizontally and integrate the retail podium into the larger development by providing access to the adjacent offices, banks and conference center.

Denver West

Denver, Colorado, USA

For the quintessential Colorado site—a steep hillside in the foothills, adjacent to a highway that connects Denver to the mountain resorts of Aspen, Snowmass, and Telluride—TrizecHahn, the developer, conducted a survey of residents and Colorado visitors to determine what they loved about the state and translated the findings into the design of Denver West. The study revealed three themes: Denver's urban lifestyle, the leisure activities in the metropolitan area and the spirit of Colorado.

Plans for the retail center reflected the individual characteristics of the residents and visitors with a unique mix of offerings. The design of the center acknowledged the findings with a Colorado aesthetic that embraced both the rough woodsy warmth of the state and the hi-tech look of the extreme sports that are a major attraction. Bridges that could be opened to breezes during the comfortable seasons joined three separate retail pavilions, surrounded by 150 feet of meadows and streams.

A western heritage museum anchored the rooftop of the central pavilion space. A major recreational outfitter utilized the incline of the site to create lakes and casting ponds for fly fishermen and water sports enthusiasts, while other outdoor venues allowed the customers to sample equipment in the natural environment. Community gatherings found a home around the large outdoor fireplaces on the site.

North Entry

Lake Galyan

Watchtower Cafe

Waterfalls

PAVILION

Entry Porte Cochère

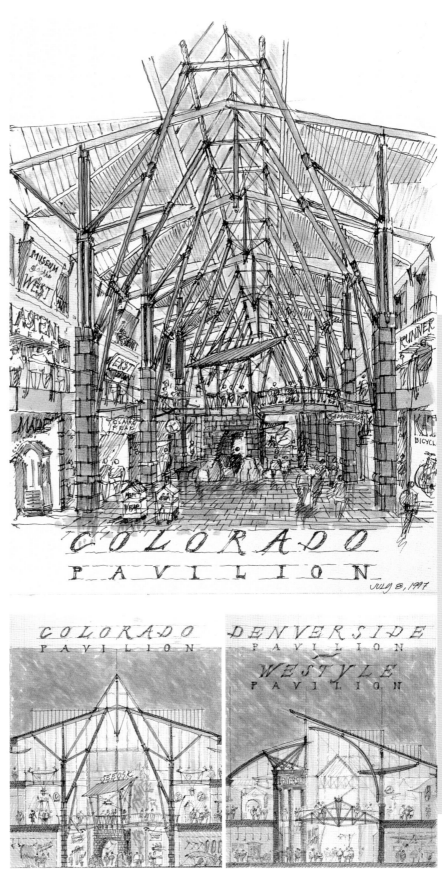

COLORADO
PAVILION

JULY 8, 1997

COLORADO
PAVILION

DENVERSIDE
PAVILION
WESTYLE
PAVILION

GO2 Town
Tao Yuan, Taiwan

GO2 Town is a major mixed-use project designed in response to the lifting of land-use restrictions in Taipei, which allowed for the development of large-scale shopping centers. By setting new standards for urban design, the complex produces a blueprint to guide future development.

The six-level center creates a highly sophisticated shopping experience for the residents of Tao Yuan City, which is located to the south of Taipei. Anchored by a five-story department store, the center features regional amenities, such as a 14-screen cinema complex, a large food court with open views, a 1000-seat banquet hall, and structured parking. These facilities are supplemented by a hypermarket and multiple restaurants.

An adjacent public park suggested that the retail spaces be placed in a garden-like setting to enhance public enjoyment. Indoor and outdoor spaces are linked by a six-story picture window so that shoppers can observe the surrounding scenery. These large, glazed surfaces gather natural light that fills the central atrium. As travelers pass along a nearby expressway, the windows provide views of the interior that communicate the vitality and energy of the spaces within.

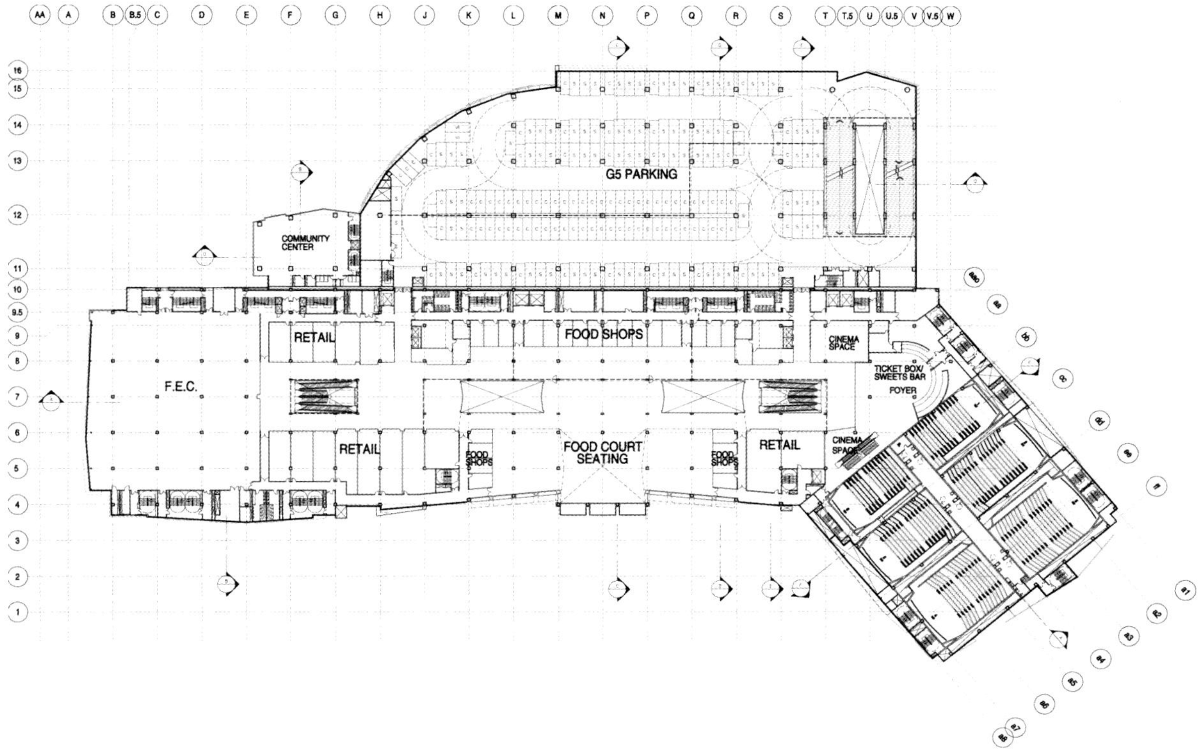
G5 PARKING
COMMUNITY CENTER
RETAIL
FOOD SHOPS
CINEMA SPACE
TICKET BOX/ SWEETS BAR
FOYER
F.E.C.
RETAIL
FOOD SHOPS
FOOD COURT SEATING
FOOD SHOPS
RETAIL
CINEMA SPACE

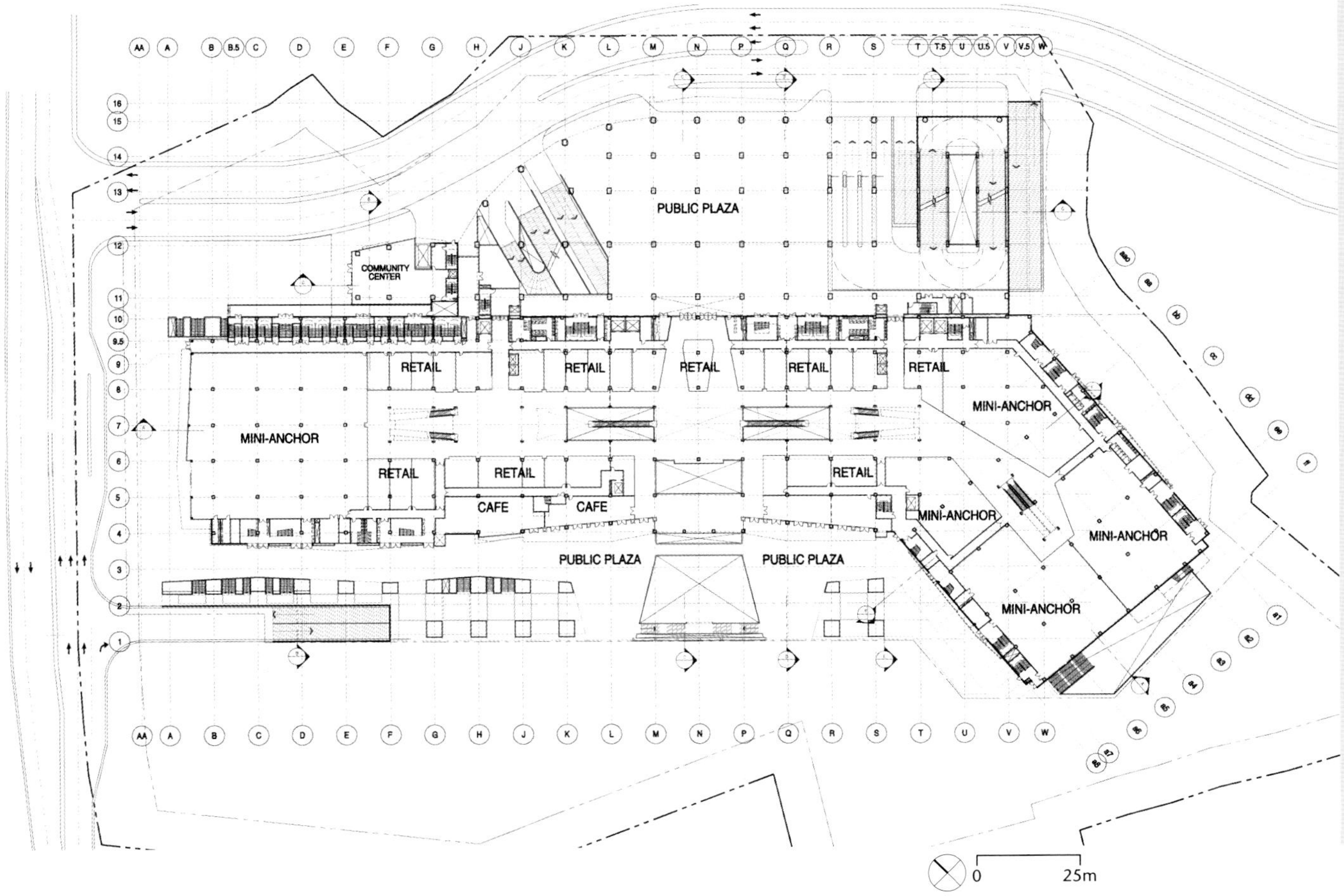
PUBLIC PLAZA
COMMUNITY CENTER
RETAIL
RETAIL
RETAIL
RETAIL
RETAIL
MINI-ANCHOR
MINI-ANCHOR
RETAIL
RETAIL
RETAIL
CAFE
CAFE
MINI-ANCHOR
MINI-ANCHOR
MINI-ANCHOR
PUBLIC PLAZA
PUBLIC PLAZA
0
25m

Guangzhou Mega Mall

Guangzhou,
People's Republic of China

Guangzhou Mega Mall, located on a major expressway that links the city of 10 million with Hong Kong and Shenzhen, provides a gateway icon for China's third-largest urban center. The city is growing in the direction of the ambitious project which captures the transformation of Guangzhou from a dreary industrial center to a modern metropolis with a contemporary image and 2.5 million square feet of shopping, leisure, recreation, dining and entertainment.

Located adjacent to the city's new 80,000-seat Olympic-class soccer stadium, and connected to the central city by light rail and the highway, the project is designed to become a landmark destination. The two-and-a-half-level scheme includes eight big-box anchor tenants, a hypermart,

12-screen cinema, 1000-seat food court, and restaurants. The design incorporates 1.5 acres of lush landscape and an array of fountains with an architecture that offers a mall, covered but not enclosed, as well as fully open courts for shopping and other leisure activities.

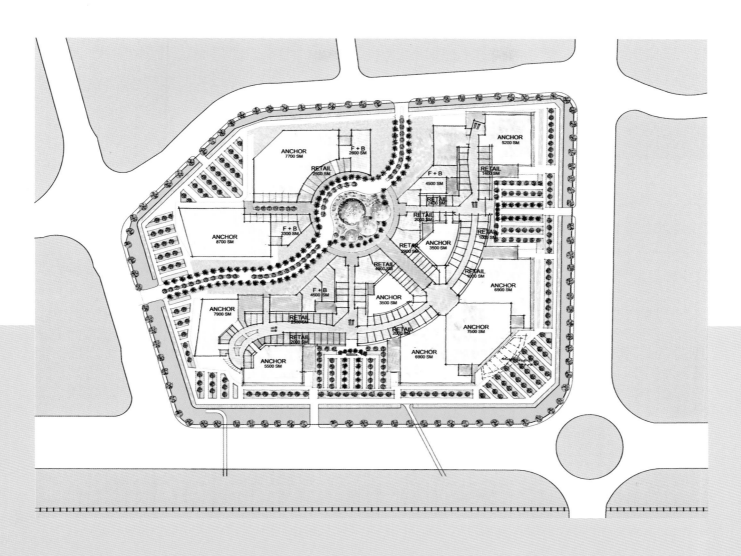

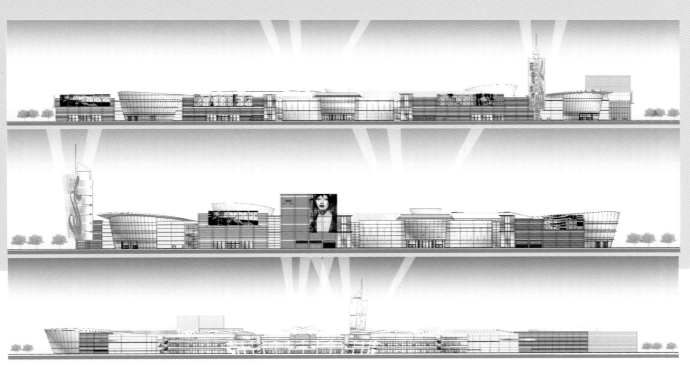

Ka'ahumanu Center

Kahului, Maui,
Hawaii, USA

The expansion of Ka'ahumanu Center repositioned the existing retail facility as an architectural landmark with a contemporary identity that embraces the island's unique climate and character. The sustainable design and construction of a second floor also increased its capacity for stores, restaurants, and amenities that appeal to both local residents and tourists.

The most striking element of the new design is a skylight that connects the interior with the island's natural environment, providing views of the sky and mountains. A translucent, fabric skylight crown spans the public space and alludes to the billowing sails of tall ships that first brought trade to the Hawaiian Islands. This design helps to conserve energy, provide ample daylight, and dissipate heat buildup by shielding the indoor spaces from ultraviolet rays.

The architects created a logo that features a regal profile of Queen Ka'ahumanu, the project's namesake, wearing a festive wedding lei. Other abstract signage motifs are based on local flora, and paving patterns reflect the play of light on the ocean's surface and coral reefs. Custom fixtures evoke the magic of native torch lights.

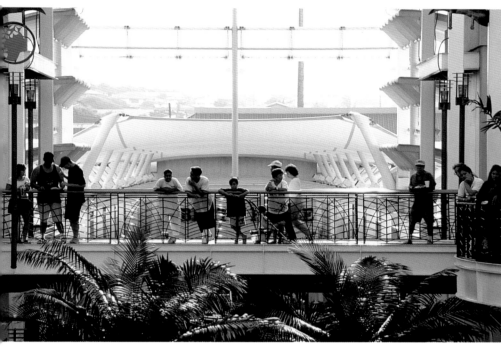

Lincolnwood Town Center
Lincolnwood, Illinois, USA

Lincolnwood, a Chicago suburb, lacked a true village center. So, when a 1.2-million-square-foot mall and office complex was proposed for the site, Lincolnwood officials were apprehensive, concerned that the new development would overpower the intimate scale that made Lincolnwood unique. However the results of this new and smaller regional destination addressed these concerns while paying homage to the suburban community's cultural roots.

Its contemporary design mixes two local architectures: the exposed structures of constructivism and the solid masonry of Chicago's civic monuments. These two styles were fused in a playful and original way, both inside and out. On the exterior façade, lightweight elements such as projecting metal canopies and a glass porte-cochère reduce the apparent density of the brick and granite walls. A double-height entrance with a large awning perched on tall columns makes for a heroic reception.

Skylights embedded in the center's gabled roof produce a generous, light-filled interior atrium with a glass elevator, escalators, a fountain, and landscaped gardens. These airy public spaces are balanced by clear sight lines and repetitive forms, which give a sense of order and discipline. Floating above the atrium, a network of trestle bridges helps visitors to navigate the space at a human scale. It also allows shoppers to experience the expansive flow of the interior as they travel from side to side and from bottom to top.

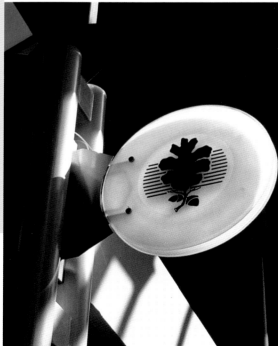

The Mall at Green Hills
Nashville, Tennessee, USA

Located in Nashville, Tennessee, The Mall at Green Hills reflects the charm and gentility of its southern home as it brings a modern vibrancy to the city. The new design converts the original conglomeration of disparate buildings into a singular shopping center that has attracted prominent merchants and upscale customers.

Elegant details and local materials helped to create a unified image for the different components that included a department store, an open-air retail strip, two single-level malls and a new 130,000-square-foot addition.

Existing details such as entry canopies and skylights were integrated into the building's contemporary façade. Other details and design cues were taken from the surrounding environment and its physical culture. Red-brick cladding recalls the rich native soil, and forest green trim refers to local building traditions. This visual order expresses a sense of permanence, coherence, and Southern grace.

In contrast to the discipline of the public façade, the interior spaces are flowing, bright, and clean. Theatrical cornices, specialty lighting and signage, and a palette of indigenous materials were carefully chosen to embrace the city's dynamic history and to represent its lively local community.

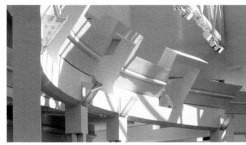

Repositioned Retail

"More important—and more difficult—in the task of recovering the relationship between place and commerce will be the task of addressing the fundamental cultural and economic characteristics of places that ultimately assure their authenticity and distinctiveness. Simply renovating structures … can serve merely to replace one form of sameness and predictability with another."

Joel Kotkin
The New Geography

Retail is a highly competitive business. Strategic location and better merchants provide certain advantages but shopping centers need to stay fresh and appealing to their customer base or they will languish. Centers can be improved with inexpensive cosmetic adjustments, however facelift renovations do not address the changes in the marketplace that contributed to the decline in business. The real opportunity lies in the transformation of a building with a negative public impression into one beloved by the community it serves.

More aggressive repositioning schemes respond to the customer's evolving expectations, recreating the center in light of new demands. Significant structural change, the replacement of dated materials and colors, the introduction of additional natural light and improved decorative lighting, and

the upgrading of the environmental graphics and internal detail elements can substantially enhance the chances for success of a new merchandising plan. Perhaps the most dramatic and challenging transformation is a second-level expansion that nearly doubles the size of an existing center and creates the opportunity for an even greater impact.

When repositioning achieves its goal, the customer has the double benefit of a distinctive, new and accommodating shopping environment in a convenient and familiar location. The latest generation of repositioned centers accomplishes even more as the newly expanded properties provide open and inviting gathering spaces that meet social and civic needs. Further, these polished and popular centers bring a sense of pride that builds customer loyalty in the communities they serve.

Alderwood Mall

Alderwood, Seattle,
Washington, USA

Rich strands of regional culture and history as well as design elements that reflect the surrounding natural environment inform the 90,000-square-foot renovation and 70,000-square-foot expansion of this regional shopping center. Design motifs from local Native American tribes and the Scandinavian fishing industry that once flourished in the area have been incorporated to create a distinctive image for the center.

The Native American colors and patterning appear in the flooring. In the food court, culturally accurate colors were selected for the totem pole colonnades, and local school children created the designs. The Scandinavian influence is notable in the food court roof, shaped like a wooden fishing vessel.

Two towers provide a backdrop for the central food court and echo the surrounding mountain ranges, the Olympics and the Cascades, while two pools reference Puget Sound and Lake Washington. Added skylights brighten the interior, create visual interest and reveal the ever-changing weather and views of the Pacific Northwest.

Arden Fair
Sacramento, California, USA

The renovation and expansion of Arden Fair in Sacramento, California, required more than an update. The 1957 regional mall needed a complete redefinition with an emphasis on its civic identity. A vertical and horizontal expansion, a renovation, and a stylistic makeover provided the transformation. The sophisticated new image of Arden Fair was created by new design elements that combined its civic traditions with the contemporary symbolism inherent in the capital city's public institutions.

References to classical and Beaux-Arts architecture were used as recurring motifs that appear in every aspect of the project, from its proportions to its details. The architects used the second-floor addition as an opportunity to insert an 85-foot, glass-canopied rotunda along the building's spine. On the outside of the building, this rotunda soars above the roof, hoisting the center back into a place of local prominence.

At the pedestrian scale, bridges help to mediate between the rotunda, the lofty ceilings, and the two levels of retail activity. To the east and west, the rotunda merges with the barrel-vaulted ceilings of two arcades. Their more intimate volumes temper the height of the interior, creating a hierarchy of grand public spaces.

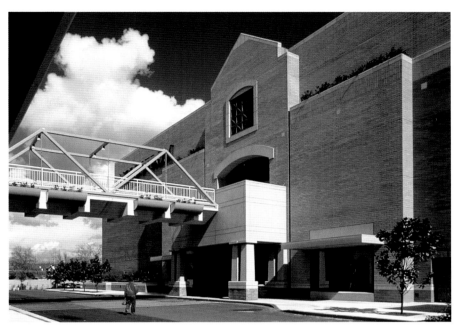

Fashion Valley Center
San Diego, California, USA

After 30 years of success, the owners of Fashion Valley Center wanted to capitalize on their asset. Upgrading the retail complex with a renovation and expansion program would appeal to a more sophisticated clientele and the upscale tourist market, and attract more upscale merchants.

Once a regional mall, the center was reborn as a 'garden cityscape' that captured the essence of the city's climate and the quality of its natural environment. The garden atmosphere was reinforced by a continuous motif of trellises, awnings and canopies and a common palette of indigenous materials such as stone, plaster, and ceramic tile. To make the shopping experience more relaxing, the rigidity of the original linear plan was replaced with smaller shopping precincts surrounded by gardens and abstract forms.

The new center provides an exciting mix of shops, terrace restaurants, a food court, and a multi-screen cinema. Fashion Valley not only offers an alternative to the city, but it also improves upon the best characteristics of its traditional urban space.

Macy*s Department Store Prototype

Roseville and Lakewood,
California, USA

In order to maximize its visibility in competitive suburban markets, the national retailer wanted a chic identity that would reposition its stores. These two contemporary and forward-looking models are helping to redefine the Macy*s image and to reconfigure its retail environment as the retailer prepares to build multiple, near-identical stores.

The new prototype balances a recognizable façade that attracts shoppers to the mall and an interactive interior that showcases the products on sale. Each design is fashioned from a lexicon of elements—such as portals, edges, and canopies—that can be reassembled on multiple sites. Planes of different materials are juxtaposed but remain physically distinct, forming a complementary mix of textures and colors. Collectively, these pieces create a series of layers that gradually pull apart, just as one opens a gift by peeling off layers of ribbon, cardboard, and tissue.

Like a gift, the design creates spontaneous experiences that elicit delight and surprise. Details are used to highlight entrances and corners, creating a sequence of arrival and movement. Glimpses of transparency draw shoppers and guide them through the store as they alternately allure, conceal, and reveal the spaces within.

Collections of Destinations

"I could not believe any Place more entertaining than Covent-Garden; *where I strolled from one Fruit-Shop to another, with Crowds of agreeable young Women around me, who were purchasing Fruit for their respective families. It was almost Eight of the Clock before I could leave that Variety of Objects."*

Richard Steele
Twenty-four Hours in London

The model for Collections of Destination is based on historic European examples—in-town shopping centers that are a fraction of the size of American prototypes. These projects are often on odd urban infill sites or bypassed suburban sites cut off by roadways. The architecture takes advantage of the unusual nature of the sites to create distinctive properties that fill a unique niche.

Scaled like village centers, these projects are designed to serve larger, more regional markets. By offering a variety of goods, including brand-name merchants that would formerly only trade in enclosed malls in suburban locations, the centers have the ability to attract customers that live beyond their immediate trade area. Desirable destinations in the centers also include local and nationally identifiable restaurants, cinemas and entertainment, civic spaces and recreational use.

The defining characteristics of the Collection of Destinations, however, are those components that cater to specific lifestyle priorities. The market is delineated by preference, not proximity. While the overall scale of the center is small by comparison, regional shopping centers feature a cross section of retail, dining and entertainment venues that are first-choice destinations for discerning customers. What are missing are the generic mall shops that have little appeal for the particular customers who fit the market profile of the center. Shoppers find an environment with a sense of intimacy and sociability that speaks in an authentic way to their locale and life choices.

Kaleidoscope
Mission Viejo, California, USA

Kaleidoscope is an oasis of activity offering dining, entertainment, and shopping in a visually exciting three-story center. Resembling a jewel in a rugged case, the project is the pearl pried from the leftovers of the Mission Viejo masterplan—a 5-acre island surrounded by the 40-foot embankments of two freeways and the backside of a strip mall. The center introduces urban values to the site with a strong pedestrian character that fosters a social ambiance by providing a town square for the South Orange community.

Kaleidoscope features a patterned plaster exterior, faceted glass panels and multicolored details. Light, used as a design element, is refracted throughout the 250,000-square-foot, three-level interior. The entire structure, crowned by a 65-foot rotunda that illuminates the night sky, serves as a beacon for the Mission Viejo business district.

The plaza level accommodates retail tenants with a large open piazza for dining and community events. The upper entertainment level has several dining terraces that overlook the piazza, as well as a ten-screen cinema complex.

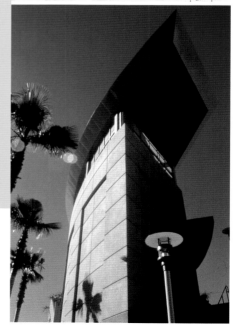

Market Square at Arden Fair

Sacramento, California, USA

Market Square recasts a bland, one-story mall as a collection of urban destinations that serve the surrounding community. A pioneering project, this retail complex creates a model for transforming aging and outdated strip malls into active urban marketplaces.

The form of the market was influenced by the lifestyles of second-generation citizens who live near Market Square. Although many of these residents were raised in California, they still maintain strong familial and cultural ties abroad. As a result, the center was designed as a Teflon-coated fiberglass skylight structure that refers to European market pavilions. In the summer, the skylight serves a practical purpose by diffusing the glare and heat of the sun. In the winter, it collects natural light, which brightens the interior spaces and warms the air.

Although the pavilion recalls a European typology, its contemporary style remains distinctively American in character. The formal scheme provides a variety of retail opportunities and the chance for playful tenant identities. Its program responds to contemporary tastes in retail and entertainment, such as a multiplex cinema, numerous restaurants, a large bookstore, and a lively music superstore.

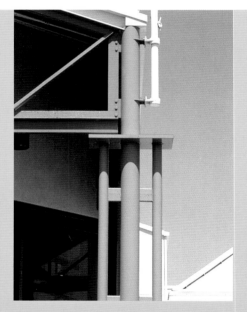

Triangle Square

Costa Mesa, California, USA

Triangle Square blends landmark-quality architecture with civic responsibility and acts as a catalyst for future development in the city's historic downtown. Located on a pivotal redevelopment site, the Square reinvents the retail hub as a true town center with a distinct urban identity, community services, public areas, and an important sense of place.

Offering a new typology for sensitive urban growth, the 200,000-square-foot project combines a fashion retail complex with a local community center on a highly visible, 4.5-acre site. Organized around an open-air piazza, the triangular slice of land accommodates a variety of different amenities, such as shops, restaurants, a supermarket, a cinema, a bank, and public parking. The elevated piazza can accommodate multiple functions, ranging from community performances to outdoor dining.

Like the hybrid program, the design mixes two regional architectural styles. The predominant Mediterranean-style vocabulary makes reference to Costa Mesa's local architectural traditions. The Colonial Revival style is used for certain signature elements such as a rotunda, an arbor, and classical colonnades.

The Waterfront, Marina del Rey

Marina del Rey, California,
USA

Set as a background to the sunny
beaches of Southern California, Marina
del Rey is strategically located at the
head of a yachting channel in the world's
largest man-made pleasure craft marina.
The Waterfront provides a place where
the resident and recreation communities
mingle, a civic space defined by the
surrounding shops and restaurants.

The project fills a social need for non-
sand public space along the waterfront
by playing to the natural attractions of
the area. Members of the community
can gather around four 'big fireplaces'
for community meetings and group
discussions, or to fry the catch of the
day. There are paths for pedestrians,
rollerbladers and bikes that lead to
coffee bars, terrace dining and myriad
booksellers and shops.

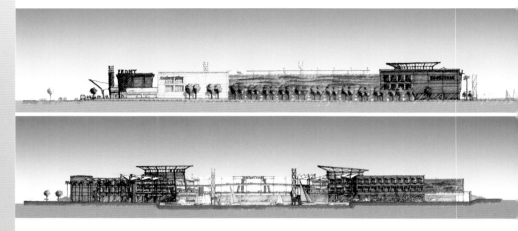

Mixed-Use

"Cities are enormously complex palimpsests of communal history and memory, a fact that tends to be obscured by their primary identity as sites of immediacy, money, power and energy concentrated on the present and the future."

Lucy R. Lippard
The Lure of the Local

Every major city was originally built on the premise of mixed-use. For centuries, the ground floor has been a public venue hosting restaurants, banks, retail shops, hotel lobbies and the show windows of department stores. Above the street, the superstructures house corporate and professional office buildings, condominium and full-rental housing, hotel occupancies, civic clubs, and entertainment venues. Configurations vary based on cultural or market preferences, but the mixed-use prototype is still being built wherever cities thrive. During 18 of the 24 hours of the day, the streets are filled with people leaving home, walking to work, shopping, conducting business, going to the theater, strolling, recreating, meeting friends, all within just a few blocks.

In post-war America, as suburban growth prevailed, uses became segregated. Work stayed downtown while bedroom communities were built a few miles outside the city. Regional shopping centers joined residential development in the suburbs, leaving downtown empty at the end of the workday. The art of building more than single-use structures was lost to developers as institutions feared financing other than the simplest project.

In the last decade, US cities have rediscovered their downtowns as new businesses and young people, seeking the vibrancy of an urban lifestyle, have returned to the city cores. As the urban renaissance spreads across America, designers and developers are once again looking at successful mixed-use models around the globe. Bustling, populous Asian cites provide excellent examples of mixed-use development with rental or condominium housing, office buildings or hotels placed in solid retail space.

Plaza Adriatico

Manila, The Philippines

Plaza Adriatico is a collection of three new residential towers that fuse with a retail galleria to create a mixed-use center that reanimates an existing complex and transforms the urban street. The phased project includes three high-rise condominiums, and three floors of retail and entertainment space. A wide pedestrian promenade, lined with a collection of restaurants, cafés, and a community 'hypermarket,' generates pedestrian movement throughout the neighborhood during the day as well as the night. The main retail entrance creates a multi-level glazed structure that sweeps customers from the promenade up to a retail center. The 700,000-square-foot retail space contains shops, cinemas, and a double-height food court that overlooks the street below.

The design of the towers brings regional landmark identity to the complex by merging clean surfaces of steel and glass with richly textured materials such as stone and tile. Each of the

1800 condominium units features oceanfront views. Set against lush tropical landscaping, the sleek buildings act as a catalyst to transform an older section of Manila into a modern oasis near the city's waterfront. The development also provides new service areas and parking for 1050 cars.

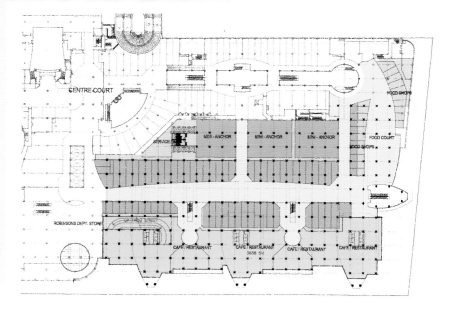

Houston Pavilions
Houston, Texas, USA

Houston, Texas has recently rediscovered the allure of its downtown as a place to live and play as well as work. In response to popular interest, a development team is masterplanning five blocks of underutilized property adjacent to the convention center, ballpark and proposed arena. In keeping with the mix of uses enjoying a renaissance, the new urban plan includes residential units, entertainment, hotels, and offices, and renovation of two adjoining blocks.

The initial move in the design intervention involves the renovation and integration of two existing city blocks, where a two-level retail component sequestered above a two-level parking structure with street frontage on all four sides served as a barrier to the rest of the site. The program for the five additional blocks called for a retail base on each block with street-edge retail to enliven the neighborhood, and a central sales spine that would link the project both internally and block-to-block. One block supports additional office space, the second a hotel, the third a cinema, and high-rise and mid-rise residential above street-level retail structures. Shops would face the street edges on all sides. Collectively, the new buildings create a district that serves the existing multi-building, multi-story offices by day and the convention center and sports venues at night.

Marina Square
Singapore

The existing mixed-use project in Singapore featured three large hotels situated above three levels of shopping, seated on a parking structure. Although the complex was in the heart of the high-identity 'Architectural District' along the waterfront and adjacent to the convention center, the retail center was invisible.

Transforming the mall, the design solution breaks open the box to give access and identity to the retail, and creates a dynamic, beehive base for the hotel towers. New materials, clear horizontal and vertical circulation, abundant natural light, consolidated food venues, and new gathering spaces energize the center. The combined retail energy is then shared with the neighboring community by virtue of a complete exterior re-imaging which included terrace overviews and two grand multi-level glazed entrances.

This visible renaissance can be enjoyed both by pedestrians along the city's major avenues, and patrons of the new cultural events center.

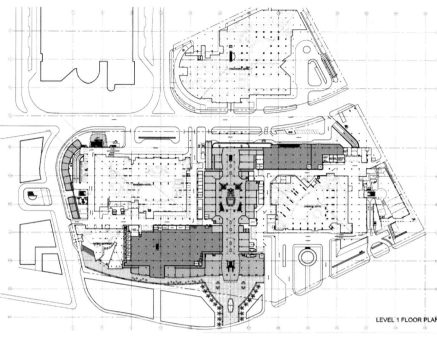

LEVEL 1 FLOOR PLAN

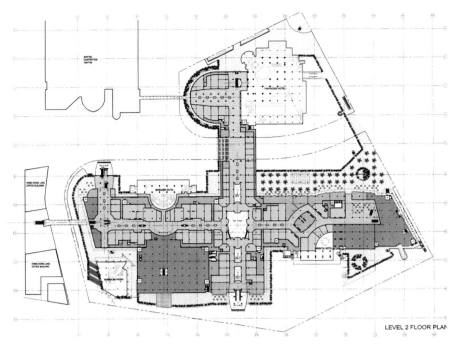

LEVEL 2 FLOOR PLAN

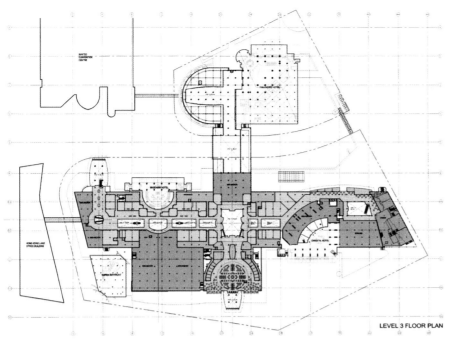

LEVEL 3 FLOOR PLAN

Taman Anggrek Mall
Jakarta, Indonesia

Southeast Asia's largest and most comprehensive retail/entertainment complex, this aggressive mixed-use center combines 2900 condominium units in eight, 36-story residential towers perched above the podium levels, housing 1.5 million square feet of retail. Located on six levels, the retail areas include a 1200-seat food court and Southeast Asia's first ice-skating rink. The center's shopping districts create linked pockets of energy that reduce the grand scale and keep visitors from being overwhelmed by the proportions.

The mall was designed as three stacked, two-level malls, each merchandised to appeal to a different market sector with a variety of other retail attractions and entertainment destinations. The first level presents High Street retail shops. The second level offers two automobile showrooms—modeled on the new generation of car boutiques in Japan. The top two levels are the 'energy floors', with food and entertainment including an international standard

ice-skating rink in a winterland annex featuring real snow, areas for virtual reality games, a six-screen cineplex, and a disco. On the fifth floor are two food courts, one featuring specialties from around the world, and Indonesia's largest domestic food market.

Parking is distributed on ten levels with a speed ramp that allows shoppers direct access to their floor of choice—a first in a region of multi-storied retail centers.

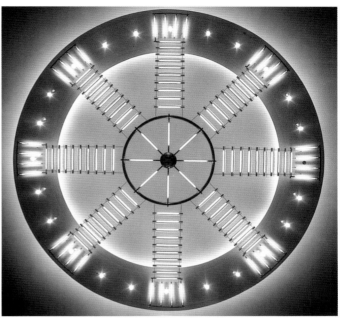

Urban Retail

Retail, in the context of urban development, benefits from the broadest definition. The components of a diverse urban retail setting include all the spaces tucked in and under office buildings, residential units, hotel and convention facilities, cultural and sporting venues, and numerous other public and private elements of the city. In this definition, urban retailing includes shops, food and beverage offerings, a wide spectrum of entertainment such as cinemas, bars and clubs, cultural and performance facilities, as well as health clubs and athletic facilities and almost any other type of interactive relationship between a physical space and its participants, be it street vendors or kiosks.

Such a broad definition can best be understood within the urban context. 'Urban' infers far more than density. Diversity, pageantry, heterogeneity, interaction, multiplicity, and continuous overlays of activity create urbanity. Streets and sidewalks, vehicles and pedestrians, patterns and textures, and people's lives give it form.

Located in a traditional city center or within an urbanized district, corridor or edge, retail activity has two dimensions—to serve and to attract. The service aspect of retail tends to satisfy a very local market. To attract, however, retail must be able to reach out to a wide geography. The ability to attract is directly related to its uniqueness, defined in terms of both the offering and its setting.

Urban retailing presents an exceptional opportunity to create the critical dimension of uniqueness.

John P. Boorne,
Chairman, CEO,
Madison Marquette

The Atrium at Kursky Station
Moscow, Russia

Strategically located at one of Moscow's major rail gateways, the building creates a sense of arrival for passengers, and gives identity to the project itself. Featuring a mix of retail, dining, leisure, recreation, entertainment, multiplex cinemas, and a winter garden, it is organized by a multi-story linear galleria and a central atrium. The highly contextual design responds to the region's harsh physical climate and to the cultural context of the urban site in Moscow.

The project, located on the Garden Ring, one of three rings on which the city of Moscow was developed, serves as a primary urban symbol and entry. The building creates an icon on the street that contributes to the historic character of the district and helps fulfill the promise that such an avenue suggests. Design details resonate with Moscow's distinctive indigenous architecture and the highly chromatic façades, providing an inviting contrast to the often-snowy streets of the city.

Inside, the winter garden offers a respite from the climate and creates a sense of order for the center. Capitalizing on the site's location at one of Moscow's multi-modal transportation hubs, the design includes key pedestrian access points and structured parking.

Mucha Centre
Prague, Czech Republic

Located at the city's main access avenue, Mucha Centre is named for a series of 26 heroic allegorical paintings by the artist Alphonse Mucha, which are incorporated into the mixed-use complex. The multi-building center is tucked behind three historic structures, which create the backdrop for the modern facilities. By incorporating old and new elements into a harmonious and respectful design, Mucha Centre contributes to the city's reputation for incomparable architectural richness.

The base of the complex forms a three-story retail galleria that is illuminated by abundant amounts of natural light. Inside, the interior spaces are arranged to link the retail spaces to other activities such as entertainment destinations, restaurants, offices and a hotel. The modern retail complex is also connected to existing public transit, outdoor plazas, and a nearby department store via a concourse system.

The Barracks, which once housed Austrian Emperor Franz Josef's troops, is converted into a five-star hotel with additional rooms atop the retail center. An office building serves the commercial needs of the burgeoning business community. Underground parking facilities provide spaces for 1000 cars.

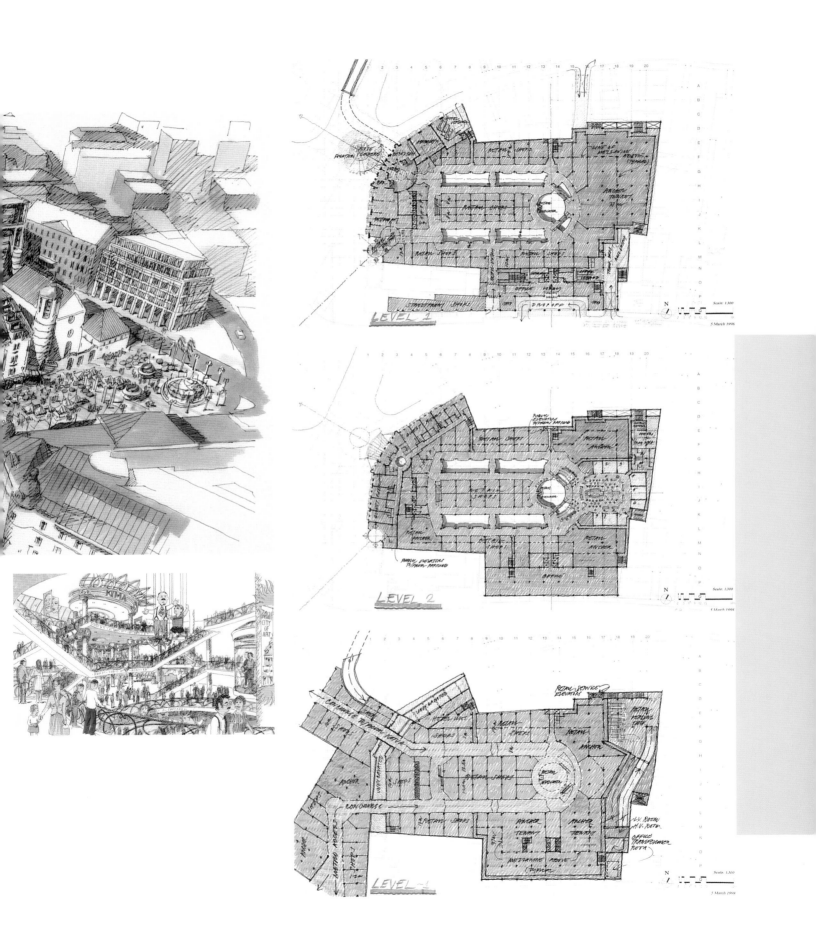

LEVEL 1

LEVEL 2

LEVEL 1

Tower Place
Cincinnati, Ohio, USA

The Tower Place urban infill development, part of a successful effort to lure customers back to Cincinnati's downtown with an upscale retail complex, functions as both a successful urban center and a cultural asset. The new building complements local traditional architecture while establishing a distinct identity. Located on a prominent 40,000-square-foot corner site, it has become a city landmark.

Tower Place has three levels of retail shops surrounding a grand skylit atrium. A distinctive art program with a suite of four paintings of civic proportion and a sculpture fountain, provide an urbane identity for the center. At street level, the shops facing the sidewalk encourage shopping along the main street.

Each of the facility's three levels connects to the landmark Carew Tower next door, providing a link to the Omni Netherlands Hotel. In its entirety, the complex consists of a 52-story office building, a 29-story hotel, a three-level retail center, and a parking garage.

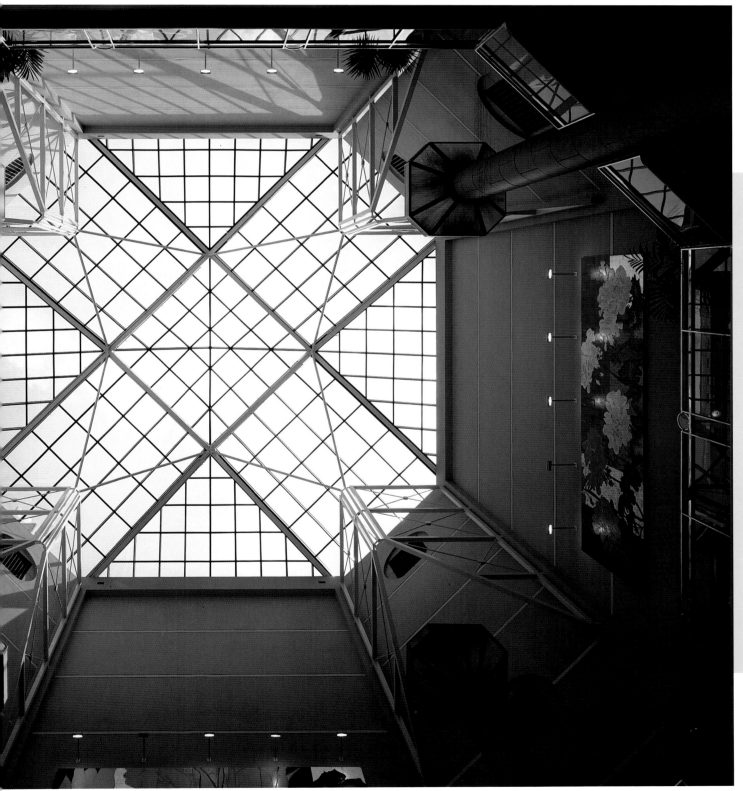

Main Street Retail

"The old, young, and everyone in between claimed Main Street as their own; it accommodated and unified them all. Outdoors and in, third place association was frequent along its short reach. The desire for a break in routine, to catch up on the gossip, or merely have something to do was as easily satisfied as a stroll uptown."

Ray Oldenburg
The Great Good Place

Main Street brought people together because it spoke, in the most articulate way, about democracy, individuality, and diverse voices. The privileged and the poor, the powerful and modest, enjoyed the same public space. With the growth of the suburbs and the arrival of the mall, Main Street was deserted. But the regional center is not community space, and the private world of the mall never filled the void left by the Main Street experience.

In recent years, shoppers have returned either to the updated originals or to projects with true Main Street values. From small single streets that connect regional malls to major roadways, to entirely new masterplanned communities, Main Street provides the framework that unifies the urban realm. It also creates a space for retail self-expression at its most unrestricted.

In enclosed regional malls, a singular architectural style establishes permanence; in Main Street retailing the contrary is true. The infrastructure of the street, the sidewalk design, the landscape, street lights, signage, water fountains, benches, newspaper and bicycle racks—the entire streetscape creates a destination that is 'city-like' rather than 'project-like.' This lively backdrop provides an opportunity for every merchant to thrive with a maximized individual identity even as they benefit from the synergy of diverse uses on Main Street. These projects are not designed as isolated fragments of the urban experience; rather they capture the full sense of downtown in a singular vision.

Kirkgate Quarter
Leeds, United Kingdom

Myriad shopping passages and gallerias define Leeds as a pedestrian-friendly town with distinctive character. The city center had suffered from decades of poor planning decisions; the introduction of a large-scale new retail development presented the opportunity to re-engineer the old Main Street infrastructure. Kirkgate Quarter, a revitalization project, builds on the urban fabric to create additional passages that link effectively to the existing pattern and connect to a historic market-hall structure and, at the same time, accommodate the modern demands of large retailers. The project connects to the regional public transport hub with a distinctive contemporary architecture that provides identity for the city's main traffic circle.

A retail area of 750,000 square feet, including a 250,000-square-foot anchor store, provides the structure that joins the historic markets, established retail arcades, and proposed

transportation interchange and leisure activities. The scheme includes two levels of retail with the anchor store extending to a third, and the winter garden that activates the area southeast of the roundabout. A strong residential component, coupled with office and hotel facilities, will make Kirkgate Quarter both a vertically integrated mixed-use project, and one that is horizontally integrated and a part of the surrounding community.

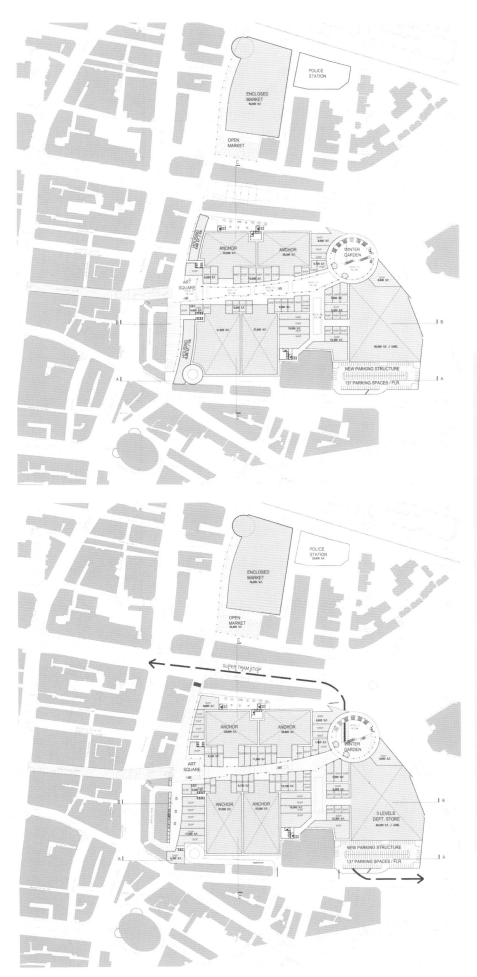

PacifiCenter @ Long Beach

Long Beach, California, USA

PacifiCenter @ Long Beach, located at the Long Beach Airport near I-405 and Lakewood Boulevard on the site of the former Boeing plant, is destined to become one of the most exciting environments for business in America. This 260-acre masterplanned campus includes 55 million square feet of office and technology space supported by two hotels, and 150,000 square feet of shops, restaurants, and services.

At the heart of the concept of diverse community lies 'The Beach', an innovative open space that overlays the ambiance of a European City Square with the raw energy of Southern California's beach. While the percentage of space dedicated to retail is relatively small, the plan envisions the shops and restaurants as the catalyst for community interaction. Retail at PacifiCenter is not a shopping center but 'Main Street'— the place where residents, workers and visitors converge to create the energy and sense of belonging that characterize strong communities around the world. And like the plaza and squares that served as models, the retail center sits in a rich public realm of tree-lined streets and green spaces to serve as the framework for the project.

Redmond Town Center

Redmond, Seattle,
Washington, USA

*American Planning Association
Honor Award Winner*

This mixed-use commercial center
masterplan provided a focal point for
the social, civic, and cultural activities
of the developing, suburban town of
Redmond. The plan included all the
amenities of a town square—a post
office, a library, banks, offices, hotel,
cinema and retail shops—in addition
to a 60-acre set-aside for a natural,
open-space preserve. Although the
project was never built, the design
garnered the American Planning
Association 1989 Honor Award.

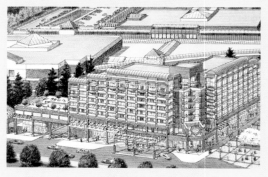

Valencia Town Center Drive
Valencia, California, USA

A pioneering Main Street project, Valencia's Town Center Drive provides a much-needed sense of place for the masterplanned community. The half-mile-long street links an existing regional mall with the community and its residents through a mix of uses that generate activity and have encouraged the redevelopment of the town's commercial district. Streetfront shops with offices above, public plazas, café dining, entertainment uses, and social spaces enrich the street and provide a sense of community highly reflective of the outdoor lifestyle and the sunny Southern California climate.

Town Center Drive, a private 53-foot-wide main street with angle parking on both sides, terminates on the east by a plaza connector to the shopping mall and on the west by a town green that connects the street to a luxury apartment complex and the adjacent country club. Along the street, the retail mix is housed in intimately scaled buildings, supporting the mall retailers by offering slightly upscale shops that cater to after-hours trade and those that have come to prefer suburban main street locations over enclosed mall space. Restaurants and entertainment venues entice residents down the street day and night. Sidewalks are 14 feet wide with pedestrian-friendly amenities such as benches, water gardens or plazas at street corners, sculptures in public places, and shade trees. With the initiation of new civic events, Town Center Drive has become a desirable and memorable public space for the community.

111

Retail Precincts

"Companies stage an experience when they engage customers in a personal, memorable way."
Joseph Pine II and James Gilmore
The Experience Economy

Rich urban environments are most often made up of distinctive commercial districts or precincts, each with a special appeal to a specific market need. Los Angeles' commercial life, for example, revolves around a variety of precincts. It boasts a Financial Center, Fashion District, Jewelry District, Government Center, Cultural Arts District, Flower District, Toy District, a Historic Theater District, and a range of areas that include China Town, Little Tokyo, Korea Town, and the historic Mexican settlement.

Taking their cue from traditional commercial patterns, retail precinct schemes acknowledge the variable preferences of shoppers. Precinct design provides a choice of environment and linkages between the different shopping areas. Options include spaces that are enclosed and air-conditioned, covered but not fully enclosed, covered but open-air, trellised, or completely open to the elements. Beyond the physical definition, precincts offer

other opportunities for distinctive identity—formal, informal, historic, and contemporary.

Culture, landscape, and other locale-specific references inform the design and the content of the environment. Precinct design creates hubs or nodes that serve as gathering spaces for promotional or community activities. From shops to outdoor cafés, fountains and shady by-ways, shoppers can enjoy a full range of social as well as commercial experiences in an afternoon of precinct exploration.

The retail precinct projects are a transitional move away from the singularity, in identity, environment and product, of large-scale regional malls and urban retail projects. They act as the forerunner of revitalized Main Street retail projects, demonstrating that the ability to offer the customer the widest possible choice in consumer goods and shopping experiences is the best way to engage shoppers and win their loyalty.

Botany Town Centre
Auckland, New Zealand

Botany Town Centre was envisioned as the civic heart of an emerging residential community in suburban Auckland. Extensive research and analysis revealed a palette of distinctive elements, experiences and relationships that form an inimitable vocabulary of place. Building on the rich regional lexicon, the Town Centre is organized as a series of distinct precincts that engage a central square with secondary squares and courtyards, connected by a system of pedestrian streets, lanes and passages. While the Town Centre's design code ensures a unified sense of place, diversity within each of the districts orients the shopper as it invites discovery.

The Town Square serves as a central focus for the precincts and provides a backdrop for the entertainment district, which includes cinemas, a food hall and a pub. From the Square, there are links to the residential community, to the Fashion District, to the Garden Walk and to a carefully proportioned, vehicular main street with professional offices above the retail base.

A conservatory creates a landmark for the enclosed fashion district. Two courtyards contain boutique shopping for Generations X and Y. The Garden Walk links convenience and supermarket shopping to household goods. Further, a bulky-goods district provides a pedestrian linkage to an adjoining retail complex, integrating the entire complex to its surroundings.

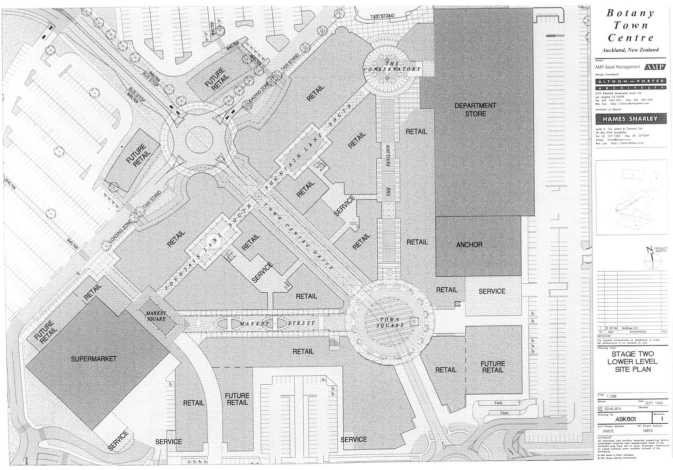

Knox City/Towerpoint Centre
Melbourne, Australia

The transformation of a regional center on the outskirts of Melbourne reshapes and re-identifies the familiar retail form by linking the center, literally and symbolically, to its context. Six separate precincts, each with a memorable name and visual personality, ease wayfinding throughout the center and offer distinct merchandising opportunities.

Knox City's locality between Melbourne and the Dandenong Ranges provides a rich pictorial and metaphorical vocabulary for the designers. The design engages the customer with an architectural evocation of the Australian lifestyle. The precincts find expression in native timbers and lodge forms, in the palette and patterns of the vineyards, broad verandas and lawns of a town square and in the bright lights and energy of the urban scene. As a result, visitors enjoy a range of leisure options and a marked sense of place that is as diverse and authentic as the region itself.

As the first phase of a long-range masterplan, Knox City Centre defines an urban framework designed to support the broad demands of community life with a mix of retail, office, civic, and residential buildings.

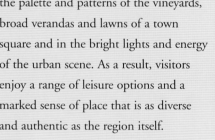

Warringah Mall
Brookvale, Sydney, Australia

Warringah Mall, built on 40 acres in a northern suburb of Sydney, had a friendly beach-side ambiance. However, the disjointed layout, the result of decades of additions with numerous designers, robbed the center of synergy. The new design brings visual clarity to the existing center and the two new wings by creating several distinct shopping precincts.

Open enough to reveal the richness of the flora and fauna of the area, the center is structured enough to give order to the circulation pattern. Taking advantage of the benign climate, the designers have created a progression of space experiences—from fully open-air to trellised, to covered yet open, to covered and enclosed, with or without air conditioning—utilizing a series of materials from fabric and glass to screens and trellises. Abstractions of architectural icons from Sydney's beaches and deserts further integrated the mall with its environment. This series of indoor–outdoor shopping

'neighborhoods,' reflecting the casual lifestyle of the Northern Beaches, are linked to the new center court with glass-covered spines. These spines allow the shopper to move from one neighborhood to another, enjoying a rich flow of experiences without losing the strong sense of place.

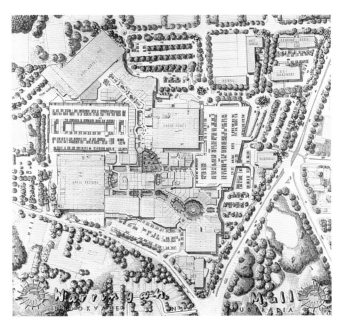

Transit Related
Retail

Transit Related Retail

"When thinking about cities, transportation and the future, it is useful to approach the subject from three vantage points. First mass transit use will go slowly ... Second, more development will be oriented toward transportation ... Third, airports are where the action will be."

William H. Hudnut III
Cities on the Rebound

Encouraged by forward-thinking municipalities, transit-oriented development—housing and commercial mixed-use—is growing up in centers along existing transportation corridors. These developments are helping to change development patterns to support extant infrastructure and control continued sprawl with its demand for more roads and utilities. However, the commercial centers at the transit stops are destined to be far more than convenient roadside malls.

Our historic memory of public transit preserves the notion of arrival at a destination of civic quality. Public use demands a public benefit. Prototypical transit villages include amenities such as child-care centers, libraries and post offices in addition to the retail and entertainment components. The retail amenities are designed to engage the transit patron in a positive and constructive way and to provide understandable linkages to the community functions. The spirit of these environments is as much civic as commercial.

In an era characterized by globalization of transactions, flexibility in production, and speed, airports are increasingly critical transit hubs. Include the security concerns of post-9/11 travel on the other demands experienced by the air traveler, and the challenge to the design of airport retail is clear. Layouts and signage that ease circulation, a healthy mix of shops and distinctive identities that create a sense of place are keys to success.

Transit-related retail is different from other models as it fulfills its civic responsibility by integrating the public and private sector functions in a development project that is coherent, community-oriented and commercially viable.

Gresham Station
Portland, Oregon, USA

Gresham Station was designed as the nexus of a carefully planned community that is located at the edge of Portland. As a transit hub, it symbolizes how the new light-rail system has helped the City of Portland to forge strong regional and cultural connections and to cultivate the linkages between its downtown core and suburban locations.

By establishing a solid development policy and creating an urban growth boundary, the city has revitalized its central core and reconnected with peripheral areas. The transit hub will energize this relationship by attracting the Portland community to visit an outlying district that was built in harmony with the natural environment. It also acts as a new gateway to Gresham, containing a variety of public amenities for local residents and visitors.

The interior space is organized around a winter garden where the primary functions of the station converge. Transportation functions are placed on the ground level with retail, cinema/entertainment, and dining spaces located above. A garden structure frames distant views of Mount Jefferson and defines an outdoor civic space. This public venue can be used for performances and gatherings such as the annual jazz festival or other community events.

Kowloon Station
Hong Kong

The first and largest stop on the new rail line connecting Hong Kong to the new airport on Lantau Island, Kowloon Center doubles as a 12-million-square-foot, mixed-use project featuring housing, hotels, office towers and retail. The design creates a retail/entertainment destination within the spatial labyrinth that forms the infrastructure of the transit system, bringing clarity with a separate identity for each of the complex's uses, and creating a civic space rare in crowded Hong Kong.

The retail podium features a city check-in counter for the convenience of regional air travelers and provides a retail/entertainment destination for local residents. Its open design directly connects the complex to the bustling street life of Kowloon. The station's modern, forward-looking aesthetic is suffused with natural light and color. The overall design is softened by sophisticated, curvilinear forms and incorporates contextual elements from Hong Kong's world-famous harbor front.

The Shops at Tanforan
San Bruno, California, USA

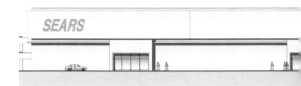

Located in San Bruno, California, 30 miles south of San Francisco and one mile north of San Francisco International Airport, Tanforan Park Mall is being transformed into a large, multi-modal, transit-oriented, mixed-use commercial center to keep pace with its changing context. The Bay Area Rapid Transit (BART) system is being extended south to a stop adjacent to Tanforan Park and a new BART station is being built on the northeast corner of the site. That facility includes a new police station for San Bruno and structured parking for 'park & ride' commuters.

The expansion of The Shops at Tanforan brings a multi-screen cinema, and additional shopping and restaurants. A new entry plaza with restaurants, cafés and a bookstore, outdoor dining and a playful water feature creates a relationship with the street. Inside, the redesigned concourses and center court create a civic space that connects to the BART station. Future focused expansion plans make provisions for the later addition of a new department store, additional new inline shops, and a new parking structure.

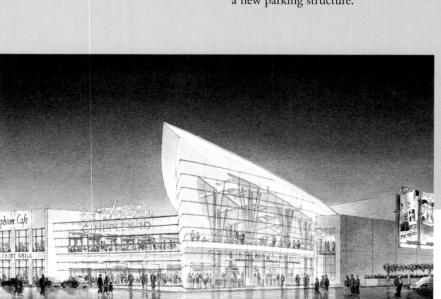

Ian Espinoza Associates

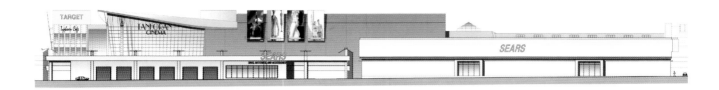

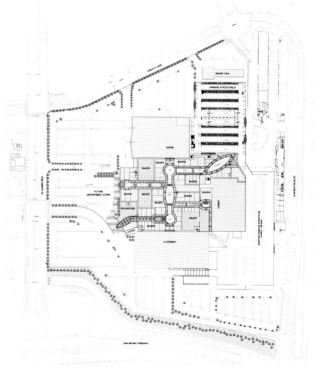

Resort Retail is the Attraction

Retail is the common element enjoyed by all resort guests. Increasingly, the retail street has become the face of the resort. The success or failure of a resort can rise or fall on the basis of its retail experience.

Great alpine, golf and beach resorts have embraced retail to enhance the visitor experience, reduce seasonality and create year-round activity. At the same time, retailers have recognized that resorts offer a captive market with a constant flow of customers. As a result, resort retailers typically experience sales performance (per foot) that is three times that of standard shopping centers.

Resort retail has been strategically used as an amenity by resort developers such as East West Partners, Intrawest and Vail Resorts to stimulate real estate sales and improve property values. By establishing fractional real estate and accommodation programs in resort villages, hotel operators including Marriott, Hyatt and Starwood have also embraced retail as a mechanism for strengthening occupancy rates and growing room rates.

Pursuit of a better lifestyle, sparked by demographic shifts and a renewed search for security and community, has resulted in many people turning to resort villages as a desirable place to live, work, shop and play. Retail has become the vital component for creating the social gathering place, which is the heart and soul of the resort.

The mixed-use resort village format, with accommodation and residences above the retail street, is now being emulated by urban communities in their efforts to recreate community at a pedestrian livable scale. Places like Paseo Colorado in Pasadena, California and the Gateway Center in Salt Lake City, have adopted the lessons learnt from resort retailing to establish the new urban gathering places, which are simply a reflection of the resort retail village experience.

Christopher LeTourneur,
Partner & Principal,
Thomas Consultants Inc.

The Gardens on El Paseo

Palm Desert, California, USA

The Gardens on El Paseo—a modern, commercial complex with retail facilities and pedestrian amenities—is the new architectural landmark of Palm Desert's premier shopping district. Located on the city's primary pedestrian street, the project fills a gap in this one-mile stretch of commercial and retail properties, creating an anchor project that the street has long been lacking.

The complex, a series of two-level buildings placed along El Paseo, embraces the pedestrian activity along the commercial corridor. A main entrance, marked by a sculpture, welcomes pedestrians. The buildings themselves are designed as simple forms with refined detailing, that use indigenous materials and rich earth colors resonant with the environmental context. They converge on the site's centerpiece—a richly landscaped plaza. Throughout, delicate trellis structures interspersed with the more solid building forms give a quiet sense of formal order. In spite of the sometimes harsh desert climate, El Paseo provides a comfortable shopping environment with the astute use of traditional forms of climate control.

The Shops at Mission Viejo

Mission Viejo, California,
USA

Mission Viejo, a bedroom community in southern Orange County, had matured economically and physically during its first generation of development. Now the aging center, an early entrant to the city's economic scene, needed a remake in a fashion more befitting the needs of the newly affluent community. Faced with a dated mall in a difficult location on a plateau above the freeway, the designers had to create a 'destination' to attract customers.

Employing dual themes of 'Resort Retail' and 'Casual Elegance', the design evolved to reflect the community's self-perception. An aura of graciousness marked by refined details speaks to the upscale lifestyle of the customers. The conversion of one department store to shops, the addition of Saks and Nordstrom, and a collection of food purveyors changed the retail mix.

The introduction of sophisticated design details and materials that recall early California architecture and the elegance of resort hotels changed the ambiance.

21st Century Prototypes

"The future is here and it is our responsibility to use it. But a leap in faith, vision and imagination is needed if we are to exploit both the advantages of natural resources and state-of-the-art technology."

Jan Kaplicky
Architecture Now

In less than two generations, the retail industry deserted downtown and became isolated in remote suburban locations. The format altered, expanded and contracted. Downtown, retail became urban intervention attached to a new mix of uses, including co-located transit centers, yet looked nostalgically backward for inspiration. Our century —the 21st—offers a fresh opportunity for the retail design imagination as newly powerful forces begin to shape the prototype.

Sustainable design is an increasingly influential factor in the architecture of retail buildings. The clear-headed practice of design as a response to the forces of the natural environment establishes a baseline. Sustainable projects of all types make strong connections between the built and the natural environment. Beyond the basics, green practice requires an investment in the intellectual capital of the organization to develop a team of specialists, from botanists to transportation engineers, who can create integrated environments that go beyond compliance to find the optimum solution.

The other challenge for contemporary architecture is the incorporation of next-generation technology into projects that are not only of their time but also of their place. Context takes on new meaning as every environment is layered with complex and evolving information. Traditional concerns, including climate, geography, landscape, and the historic environment, still matter. Retail design must also consider infrastructure, economics, the social environment of ethnicity, culture, religion, and customs and the human environment of perception, reality, comfort, joy, and memory.

Retail architecture must respond to these imperatives to maintain its place on the forward edge of invention because, after all, that is the very essence of the retail experience.

Auchan
Suburban site, Italy

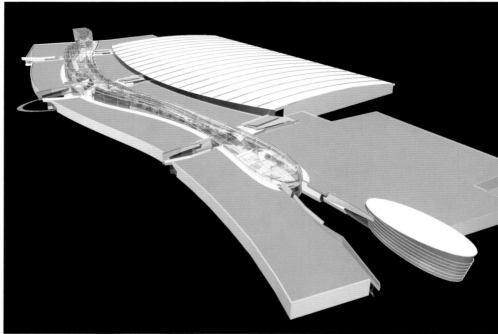

The Italian hypermarket company, Auchan, recognized that while its highly popular stores were retail success stories, they contributed little to the sense of community in the vast regional centers they served. As a remedy, Auchan sponsored an international design competition with an emphasis on the concept of retail center as placemaker.

Shopping is movement. The design response recognized that the architecture of the retail experience is based on the passage of shoppers with and against the grain of the building by employing two distinct vocabularies of form and space. The smooth, linear composition of the building's central seam emphasizes continuous, dynamic movement along the transverse access. Five fractured gaps break the exterior shell to imply erratic, rapid movement as a transitional experience between the outside and inside. The new and unmistakably 21st-century icon recasts the dowdy building prototype as an enlightened and invigorating experience.

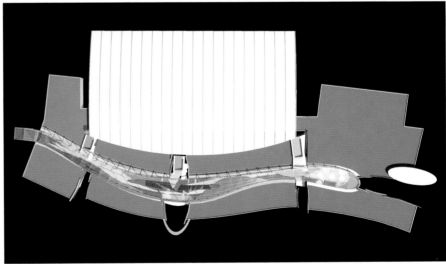

Chodov Centrum
Chodov, Prague,
Czech Republic

A vibrant, 21st-century community located outside of Prague, Chodov reaffirms the triumph of democratic values in a former communist country. As a symbol of the political and social changes that have taken place in the past decade, the new development reinvigorates a Soviet-inspired housing complex that was never fully built. It also adds the right mix of ingredients to make a successful neighborhood, such as civic, retail and residential spaces that are replete with historic references and contemporary grace.

The organic plan softens the austere architecture of the existing residential structures and enhances pedestrian movement throughout the reactivated urban realm. The retail program forms a circulation system that passes through a sequence of varied public spaces and inspires inquisitive search. At the base of the four-story complex, the project is linked to the subway system and a transit concourse with amenities such as a hypermarket for community use. Above, the roof features a large garden, a dining facility and a cinema. This elevated platform affords panoramic views of the Czech countryside that surrounds the new development.

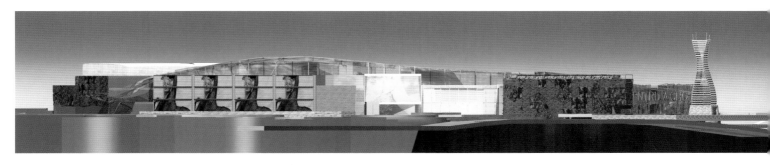

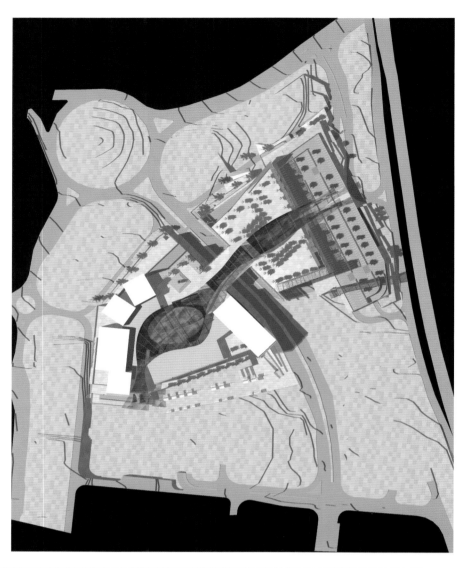

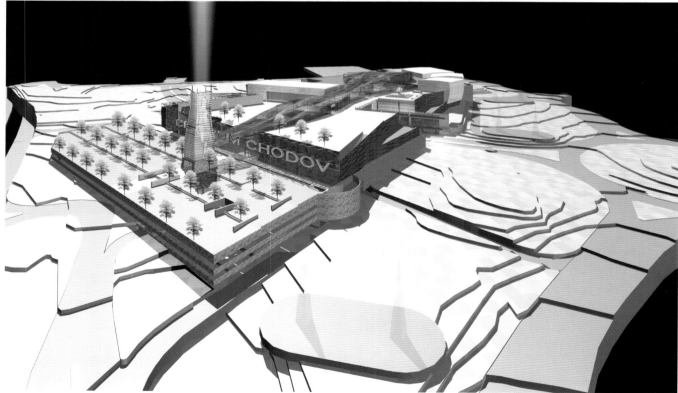

Fashion Show
Las Vegas, Nevada, USA

The remake of Fashion Show doubles its already 1-million-square-foot size, expanding from a five-department-store regional shopping center to an eight-department-store center. But it is not only the additional space and stores that are destined to reposition the Fashion Show. The Rouse Company, the current developer of the 20-year-old mall, is taking its story to the Strip, where it capitalizes on the evolving pedestrian nature of the street.

The design for the expansion takes its cue from the name and content of the Fashion Show. Instead of a theme, the center establishes its presence with a large, high-tech structure known as The Cloud. Suspended 180 feet in the air above a 72,000-square-foot plaza just off of Las Vegas Boulevard, The Cloud provides visual entertainment, shade and an iconic image for the mall. Beneath the structure, a sophisticated audio-visual system projects images to and from the plaza and the cloud with a series of super-sized LED screens.

Fashion shows from around the world and within the building itself are projected as they take place in real time. The system allows the mall to change the message with the swiftness of current fashion trends. Inside, a great hall, 850 feet in length and 150 feet wide, gives shoppers the chance to watch real fashion shows on an elevated runway/stage.

The design provides the perfect promotional platform for the Fashion Show, for the retailers, and for the brands that can create lifestyle fashion events in a flexible venue that gives an exceptional level of intimate customer contact. With 1,000 feet of frontage on the Strip telling the story, the developer expects to attract a larger share of the local and tourist markets, especially international visitors.

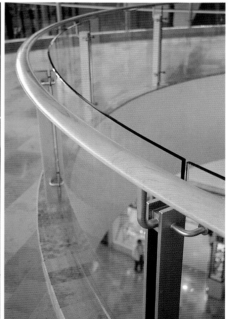

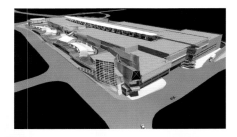

Setú Centre
Setúbal, Portugal

Setúbal, a seafront town with warm, small-scaled Mediterranean buildings built into a hillside, was an historic point of demarcation in the 15th century. In the 21st century, the design for this site acknowledges the contribution of those Portuguese explorers who looked beyond the horizon to new opportunities.

A large hypermarket store anchors the project while a retail mall set perpendicular to the store's axis allows the widest possible display of merchandise from end to end and, at the same time, provides convenient parking. Parallel to the indoor mall, is a second space with a civic nature that fronts the street of the adjoining neighborhood. The outdoor area, sited to take advantage of the cooling sea breezes, creates an environment that could never happen in a traditional hypermarket center—a place where customers can congregate, dine and promenade.

The scheme transforms the expectation of the retail center as it utilizes the magnetic attraction of the hypermarket to draw in customers then surprises them with an unexpected sense of community in exchange. Setú Center plays on the notion of discovery, both as a shopping and a social experience.

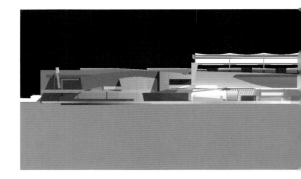

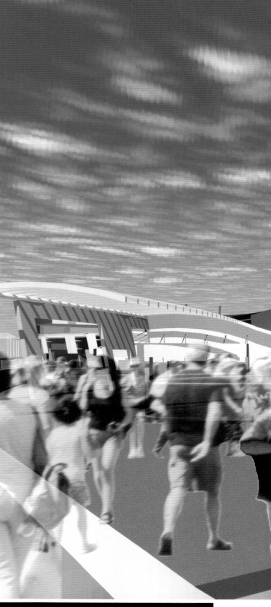

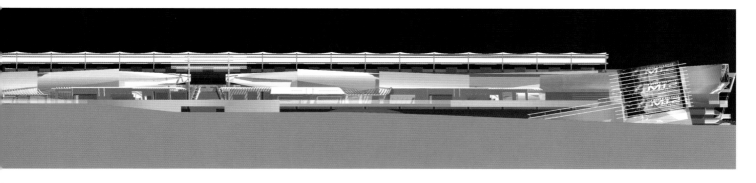

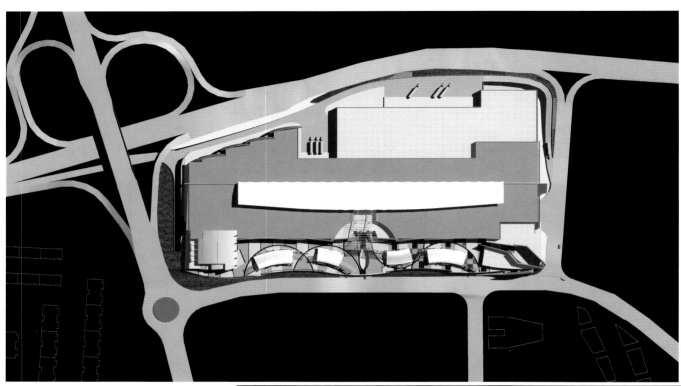

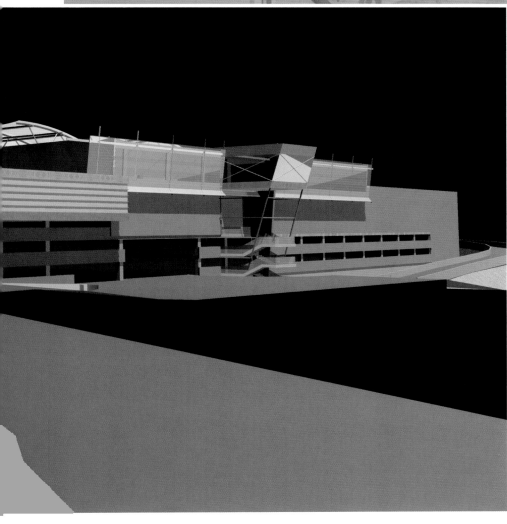

Victoria Gardens

Rancho Cucamonga,
California, USA

In a dramatic seachange for the retail industry, Victoria Gardens is seen not as a project, but as a town that reflects the values of a multi-generational community with a strong sense of urban precedence. The design for this 1.2-million-square-foot project is rooted in the elements common to all towns, and in the special qualities of the singular place. Planned around a grid of multiple streets, a town square, courtyards, paseos, pocket parks, and plazas, the individuality of shops and buildings thrives on a sense of order in the urbanscape and dissonance among the individual building designs.

Two-story retail shops, second- and third-floor office space, and residential lofts above retail, all create a scale necessary to achieve a sense of cityscape. Civic uses such as a large children's performing theater, conference center, and central library, all located around a civic square, bring institutional quality to the community. An adjacent residential community contiguous to the site reinforces the town setting. Located on a gently sloping site, the natural grade underscores a sense of authenticity. The landscape and urbanscape elements add distinction and differentiate one street from another.

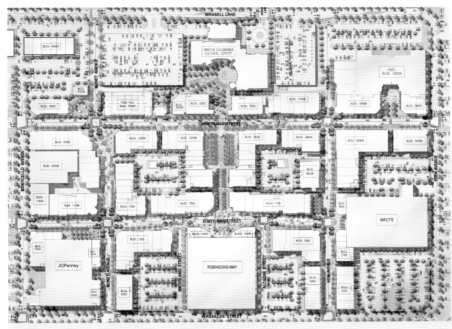

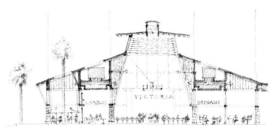

Sustainable Design of Retail Environments

The design of large-scale commercial retail environments is much like urban design: creating the context and fabric within which individual elements (in this case, retail stores) can exist and flourish. The concept of sustainability is broadly applicable to such projects—starting with the project's impact on urban infrastructure and going all the way down to the environmental design criteria for individual shops. Some of the ways in which 'green design' criteria can impact and benefit a large-scale retail project are demonstrated by the Altoon + Porter projects in this book.

Sustainability in retail is typically about people, economics, and environmental responsibility. They are all important, but of course a retail space that doesn't cater to people will not be financially successful, so the other goals never get a chance to matter. Happily, there is a way to do all three at once.

People
People desire appealing, exciting, comfortable spaces to be in and to be seen in, to meet, to shop, to hang out. This requires good design first, but there is strong evidence that designed environments, which successfully integrate sustainability features, will be more appealing to people and thus will be more economically successful. These sustainability features focus on good indoor environmental quality (IEQ), which includes indoor air quality (IAQ), lighting/daylighting, thermal comfort, humidity control, acoustics, and odor control. For example, daylight in retail spaces has been shown to positively impact retail sales by as much as 40 percent.[1] In addition, it allows the use of less electric lighting during daytime hours, which reduces energy costs and environmental impacts from electricity production. The integration of day-lighting into the architectural design of a retail environment is a hallmark of good design.

Economics
The primary economic indicator of a successful retail environment is its sales volume per square foot, and this can be significantly affected by various IEQ factors, as described above. The other economic aspect is the control of costs,

1   Study by The Heschong Mahone Group for Pacific Gas & Electric Co., *Impacts of Daylighting on Retail Sales*, 1999, www.h-m-g.com/Daylighting/

for constructing and for operating the facility, including energy costs, and operating and maintenance (O&M) costs. Traditionally, retailers have been very focused on keeping construction costs down, and this is still true. However, there is a growing recognition that sustainability features and systems can be incorporated into standard budgets, and that designs which can deliver the desired impacts on people will more than pay for themselves.

Environmental Responsibility

The buying public is increasingly aware of and interested in the environmental impacts of the products and services that they buy. This has strongly influenced the goods that are sold as well as the designs of the buildings in which they are sold. Good sustainable design of their facilities offers retailers the opportunity to be responsive to this in ways that are also good business. Thus, the trend is toward designing retail environments that not only deliver environmental benefits, but which also document and promote the sustainability story. Most notably this has led to the development of an application guide for the LEED™ green building rating system specifically applied to retail facilities.[2] Whether or not retailers elect to tout the sustainability of their facilities, they are choosing to make them green because it is good business and good citizenship.

Integrated Design is the Key to Cost-Effective Sustainable Design

All of these aspects of sustainable design must be delivered by the project team using an integrated design approach if it is to be done successfully and cost-effectively. This must necessarily be led by the architect, who is responsible for both establishing the business case for the building with the owner and for orchestrating the successful design implementation by the project team.

Elements of Sustainable Design

Sustainable design deals with five major categories: site, energy, water, indoor environmental quality, and materials. Each of these topics presents major opportunities and challenges for designing large-scale retail environments. Successful sustainable design addresses each of these, selecting from a palette of concepts and principles. No two projects are alike, and it is fascinating to see how applying these principles and concepts in varying ways to different retail projects produces such strikingly different results. Successfully applying them generally involves addressing questions such as:

Site

At the largest scale, what are the transportation impacts? How accessible is the site to existing transportation corridors, and to alternative public transportation? How can site lighting be effective in setting mood and providing security while also respecting issues of night sky pollution and light trespass to neighboring areas? How can storm water runoff be controlled and minimized?

Energy

How can comfort be achieved while also controlling energy and operating costs? What kind of high-performance glass can be used that also allows good visibility for retail displays for passersby? What are the trade-offs between central energy systems and metering and reducing overall energy usage in the mall and shops?

Water

Can reclaimed water be used for irrigation, water features, toilets, etc? How can water needs for irrigation be minimized while still providing appealing outdoor environments?

Indoor Environmental Quality

How to ensure maximum daylight in the stores and public spaces? How can natural ventilation be used to provide better indoor air quality and to minimize energy costs? How can shading, wind screens and materials colors be used to mitigate the extremes of the local climate? In an enclosed mall, how to create a light, airy interior circulation space that is economical to light, heat, cool, and ventilate? In an outdoor mall, how to provide transitions from outdoors to indoors which are both inviting and energy-efficient?

Materials

For renovation projects, can existing materials be reused? If so, how to maximize reuse of the existing structure and systems while still accomplishing the desired modernization and expansion? What sustainable materials (high recycled content, low toxics) can be used?

Dr Malcolm Lewis, PE
President, CTG Energetics, Inc.,
Irvine, California

---

2   See draft *LEED Application Guide for Retail*, US Green Building Council, 2002, www.usgbc.org
LEED™ stands for *Leadership in Energy and Environmental Design*, and is the green building rating system published by the USGBC.

Botany Town Centre
Auckland, New Zealand

Botany Town Center is a mixed-use project that includes office, retail, entertainment, dining, and links to adjoining residential communities and civic functions. It is served by regional and local buses. Working closely with environmentalists, the designers achieved high marks for the sensitive incorporation of stormwater management, light-production reduction, water-use reduction, optimized energy performance, use of local and regional materials, low emission materials, daylight and views.

New Zealand's National (multi-modal) Pathway was re-routed to pass through the project site, to encourage alternative transportation arrivals. There is also bicycle storage, and lockers and showers for employees who cycle to work. Working with the New Zealand National Arboretum, the center acquired culturally significant but endangered flax plant specimens to create an on-site flax arboretum for traditional use by indigenous people. Landscape planners also selected several flowering and fruiting trees and vines and negotiated with local service clubs to pick and deliver the flowers and fruit to senior centers. Even the artwork is sympathetic to the environment as the Kauri tree, one of the rainforest's most sacred trees, is depicted within the conservatory.

The Gardens on El Paseo

Palm Desert, California, USA

Developer: Madison Realty Partnership, Cincinnati, Ohio

The Gardens, a two-level open-air retail complex, capitalizes on traditional methods of making the desert climate hospitable. Six paseos, tight high-wall spaces, use trellises to create light and shadow. The project maximizes open space with softscape or natural desert floor material. A desert garden at the front of the project provides water retention, allowing for stormwater run-off and water treatment on site. Bosques of palms reduce the impact of heat, while the pavers, set in sand on both levels, may be watered down in the mornings to create an enhanced microclimate through slow evaporation. The use of indigenous, water-efficient landscaping also reduces water consumption.

The use of local materials, including integral color stucco, reduces the need for repainting surfaces. The project, including the department store, is entirely daylit. More than 50 percent of the parking is covered and additional deck-top parking is trellised to help mitigate sun exposure.

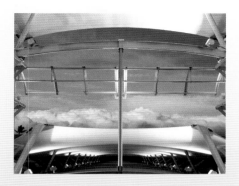

Ka'ahumanu Center
Kahului, Maui, Hawaii, USA

The design of Ka'ahumanu Center uses Teflon-coated fiberglass material for a roof that provides rainwater protection yet allows the Kona and trade winds to alternately blow through the project, eliminating the need for air conditioning the large common area. Additionally, the translucent fabric admits 70 percent of ambient daylight, eliminating the need for energy-consuming lighting during all but the after-dusk hours. The innovative skylight system is designed to reduce the heat island effect in all common public areas. One hundred percent of the space is daylit and views to the surrounding mountain ranges and the ocean are available throughout the center.

The use of Teflon-coated fiberglass for the roof resulted in virtually no debris that had to be removed from the site for the largest single constructed portion of the project. The life cycle of the material is such that re-roofing will not be necessary for at least a 30-year period, if not more. On the ground, pavers are set in sand so that wind-borne water entering the project can be absorbed and retained at the site.

The following past and present employees of Altoon + Porter helped to make the projects in this book a reality.

We have made every effort to ensure that the names are complete and correct, but we apologize for any errors or omissions. Our thanks to all of the following people:

Partners:

Ronald A. Altoon, FAIA

James F. Porter, AIA

Harvey R. Niskala, AIA

Gary K. Dempster, AIA

Carl F. Meyer, AIA

William J. Sebring, AIA

Randy C. Larsen, AIA

James C. Auld, Jr., AIA

Evelyn Abramson

Leticia Aclan

Vivien Adao

Dale Addy

Emily Altoon

Eric Altoon

Ryan Altoon

Bryoe Ambrazienas

Stephen Andrews

Paula Arviso

Troy Auzenne

Vaughn Babcock

Darlene Bailey

Theresa Baker

Jason Balinbin

Darrell Bandur

Gaila Barnett

Thomas Bastis

Jeffrey Bautista

JoDee Becker

Ronald L. Benson, AIA

Humberto E. Bermudez

Tina Bernardo

Erlinda C. Berrios

Giovanni Bignasca

Chrissie Blaze

Dee Ann Bollow

Andre P. Briscoe

Guy Matthew Buckles, AIA

Arthur D. Buczek

Rafael Caballero

Ellen Cabrerra

Ruben Catabas

Sandra Cervantes-Caraballo

Ian Cha

Fandi Yuen Yi Chan

Margaret T. Cheung

Donna Chinchar

Jin Chun

E. Cialic

Dan Cockrell

Rosie Contreras

Alison Covert

Romulo Cruz

Timothy C. Cruz

Binh T. Dang

Ann Davidson

Delores Deck

Michael Delaney

Adriana Donea

Suzanne Dvells

Marjan Ebrahimi

Moon Song Empig

Paul H. Enseki, AIA

Layla Eyermann

Leslie Fernald

Diego Fernandez

Nidia Figueroa

Jeff Fineman

Julie Flattery

Hillary Fleischer

Maria Flores

Jack Fong, AIA

Susan Ford

Cindy Fox

Aida Gabaldon

Art Garcia

Victor A. Garcia

Marvin Ginsberg

Robert Glennie

Ian Gold

Erwin Gomez

Hector Gomez

John Gormley, AIA

Barrington Gowdy

David Green, AIA

Delphine Gregoire

David Greunke

Kenneth Grobecker, AIA

Eva Gryczon

David W. Hall

Megan Hamlin

Phillip Han

James Hansen, AIA

Antoine Harb

Tracey Hardwick

Tiffany Hartley

Lori Ann Hashimoto

Andre Helfenstein

Jane Hendricks

Glen Anthony Hensley

Jessica S. Hensley

Hans Herst

Cindy Hoebink

Shannon Holderman

William Huang

Ronald J. Hutchens, AIA

Matthew Imadomi

Maryati Imanto

Matthew Inadomi

Stephen Ip

Chacko C. Jacob

Charles Johnson

Mohan Joshi

Kevin Joyce, AIA

Arlene S. Juan

Peter Jung

C. Karung

Louis A. Kaufman, AIA

Greg Keating

Robin Kerper

Frederick P. Kerz, AIA

Kazuhiro Kibuishi

Joshua L. Kimmel

Jeanne Kinney

Ann M. Knudsen, AIA

Mary Kopitzke

Gary G. Krenz, AIA

Pamela Ku

Richard L. Kuei

Hendra Kusuma

Daniel Kwok

Julie Lamprecht

Kim Landau

Alison Larsen

Masi Latianara

Mitchell Lawrence, AIA

Charles Lee

Manki Lee

Stella Lee

Raymond Leung

Jill Lewis

Paul Li

Chin K. Lim, AIA

Eric H. Lin

I-Joen Lin

Fang Liu

Kenneth R. Long, AIA

Nancy Long

Chen Lu

Frank Lu

Rny Madale

Christine Magar

Daryl M. Maguire, ANZIA

Klayden Malekpourani

Steven McEntee

Carmel McFayden

Kenneth McKently

Sabrina Medrano

Gaylord Melton

Angela Mercer

Carinne Meyer

Colette Meyer

Douglas B. Meyer, AIA

Frederick Meyer

Neelam Mian

Ellen Miller

Blythe Million

Hiroko Miyake

Catherine D. Morado

Yunjoo Namkoong

Matthew Nelson

Alleta Nesbit

Lourdes Nishi

Michelle Niskala

Cindy Ng

Ung Ngu

Charles W. 'Duke' Oakley, FAIA

John Oda

Steven S. Oh

Michael J. O'Sullivan, AIA

Mark Owen

Monica C. Owen

Benjamin Oyeka

Jane Paget

Cindy Panameno

Tiffany Pang

Lisa Park

Young Adam Park

Angelito Pasamonte

Purnima Patil

Cynthia Phakos

John Phung

Jose Pimental

Marco Polanco

Trevor Pollard

Arran Porter

Damon Porter

Beverly Powell

Mohan Pradhan

Evelyn Prinz

Maria Quandt

A. Racho

Jerome Radin

Mark Randolph

David Reddy, AIA

Tom Robertson

Edward Robison

Youngjoo Roh

Maria Romero

Tymon Ros

Brian Russell

Kate Russell

Francine Sacco

Karen Safer

Tim Sakamoto

Yasuyuki Sakurai

James Salazar

Sonal K. Sancheti

Shahan Sanossian

Ricardo Santia

Kristi Schneider

Jeffrey Schneider

Margaret Schwartz

Andrew Scott

Linda Scott

Leonarda Seward

Mark J. Shaw

JoAnn Sheu

Artin T. Simonian

Marta Recio Slagter

Amy Smith

Andie Squires

Olesia Stefurak

Andrea Stein

Yingzu Su

Fay Sveltz

Chiuling Ta

Annie H. Tan

Kanit Tantiwong

Ruben Torres

Diemmi Tran

Paul Tran

Anne Trelease

Charles C. Tsai

Julia Tschiersch

Lisa Tucker

Ung Ngu

Shigeru Usami

Manuel J. Vargas

Jon W. Vaszauskas

Frank C. Ventura Jr.

Suzy Vernoff

Huey Vuong

Sylvia Wallis

Kevin Ward

Eva Waters

Evette Westbrook

Glenn Williams

Anna Win, AIA

Joanna W. Wong

Marilyn Wong

Annette Wu

Danielle S.N. Yafuso

Libing Yan

Liming Yang

Nushin Yazdi

Bill Yee

Chien Yeh

Julian Yip

Leslie J. Young

Megan Younger

Ivy W. Yung

Michael Zakian

Hraztan Zeitlian

Min Zhu

Photography and architectural
illustration credits:

Plaza Adriatico
Manila, The Philippines
Architectural illustrator: Scott Lockard,
Lockard Creative, Kentfield, California

Alderwood Mall
Seattle, Washington
Photography: Michael Ian Shopenn,
Michael Shopenn Photography,
Port Townsend, Washington
Ronald A. Altoon, FAIA

Al Mamlaka at Kingdom Centre
Riyadh, Kingdom of Saudi Arabia
Photography: Joe Poon, Riyadh,
Kingdom of Saudi Arabia

Arden Fair
Sacramento, California
Photography: Jane Lidz, Jane Lidz
Photography, San Francisco, California

The Atrium at Kursky Station
Moscow, Russia
Photography: Ronald A. Altoon, FAIA

Botany Town Centre
Auckland, New Zealand
Photography: Grant Sheehan,
Grant Sheehan Architectural
Photographers
Michael Ng, Sitework Photography
Ronald A. Altoon, FAIA

Denver West
Denver, Colorado
Architectural illustrator: Communication
Arts, Denver, Colorado

Fashion Show
Las Vegas, Nevada
Photography: Erhard Pfeiffer,
Erhard Pfeiffer Photography,
Los Angeles, California
Ronald A. Altoon, FAIA

Fashion Valley Center
San Diego, California
Photography: Erhard Pfeiffer,
Erhard Pfeiffer Photography,
Los Angeles, California
David Hewitt/Ann Garrison,
David Hewitt/Ann Garrison
Architectural Photography,
San Diego, California

The Gardens on El Paseo
Palm Desert, California
Photography: Erhard Pfeiffer,
Erhard Pfeiffer Photography,
Los Angeles, California
Ronald A. Altoon, FAIA

The Mall at Green Hills
Nashville, Tennessee
Photography: Timothy Hursley,
Little Rock, Arkansas
Ronald A. Altoon, FAIA

Gresham Station
Portland, Oregon
Architectural illustrator:
Hank Hockenberger,
Long Beach, California

Guangzhou Mega Mall
Guangzhou, People's Republic of China
Architectural illustrator: Barry Zauss,
Barry Zauss Associates, Beverly Hills,
California

Houston Pavilions
Houston, Texas
Architectural illustrator: Alex Kosich,
AIA, Tehachap, California

Ka'ahumanu Center
Kahului, Maui, Hawaii
Photography: David Franzen,
David Franzen Photography,
Kailua, Hawaii
'Exterior at Night' photo courtesy
of Birdair

Kaleidoscope
Mission Viejo, California
Photography: Erhard Pfeiffer,
Erhard Pfeiffer Photography,
Los Angeles, California
Ronald A. Altoon, FAIA

Kirkgate Quarter
Leeds, United Kingdom
Architectural illustrator:
Peter M. Hasselman, FAIA, Orinda,
California

Knox City/Towerpoint Centre
Melbourne, Australia
Photography: Stuart Curnow,
Curnow Photography, Melbourne,
Australia
Ronald A. Altoon, FAIA
William J. Sebring, AIA

Kowloon Station
Hong Kong
Architectural illustrator: Scott Lockhard,
Lockard Creative, Kentfield, California

Lincolnwood Town Center
Lincolnwood, Illinois
Photography: Don DuBroff,
Don Dubroff Photography,
Chicago, Illinois

Macy*s Department Store Prototype
Roseville and Lakewood, California
Photography: Erhard Pfeiffer,
Erhard Pfeiffer Photography,
Los Angeles, California

Market Square at Arden Fair
Sacramento, California
Photography: Cathy Kelly,
CK Architectural Photography,
Sacramento, California

The Shops at Mission Viejo
Mission Viejo, California
Photography: Erhard Pfeiffer,
Erhard Pfeiffer Photography,
Los Angeles, California
David Hewitt/Ann Garrison,
David Hewitt/Ann Garrison
Architectural Photography,
San Diego, California

Mucha Centre
Prague, Czech Republic
Architectural illustrator:
Peter M. Hasselman, FAIA,
Orinda, California

PacifiCenter @ Long Beach
Long Beach, California
Architectural illustrator: Ian Espinoza,
Ian Espinoza Associates, Glendale,
California

Redmond Town Center
Redmond, Washington
Architectural illustrator: Carlos Diniz,
Carlos Diniz Associates Visual
Communications, Los Angeles,
California

Taman Anggrek Mall

Jakarta, Indonesia

Photography: Erhard Pfeiffer,
Erhard Pfeiffer Photography,
Los Angeles, California

The Shops at Tanforan

San Bruno, California

Architectural illustrator: Ian Espinoza,
Ian Espinoza Associates, Glendale,
California

Tower Place

Cincinnati, Ohio

Photography: Greg Matulionis,
Greg Matulionis Photography,
Cincinnati, Ohio
Rick Alexander, Rick Alexander and
Associates, Inc., Charlotte, North
Carolina

Triangle Square

Costa Mesa, California

Photography: Paul Bielenberg,
Paul Bielenberg Photography,
Hollywood, California

Valencia Town Center Drive

Valencia, California

Photography: Erhard Pfeiffer,
Erhard Pfeiffer Photography,
Los Angeles, California
Ronald A. Altoon, FAIA

Victoria Gardens

Rancho Cucamonga, California

Digital renderings: Liquid Light Studios

Warringah Mall

Sydney, Australia

Architectural illustrator:
Peter M. Hasselman, FAIA,
Orinda, California
Photography: Stuart Curnow,
Curnow Photography, Melbourne,
Australia
Ronald A. Altoon, FAIA

The Waterfront

Marina del Rey, California

Architectural illustrator: Alex Kosich,
AIA, Tehachap, California

We have made every effort to ensure that the names are complete and correct, and apologize for any errors or omissions. Our thanks to all of the following people.

Plaza Adriatico
Client: Robinsons Land Corporation
Associate architect: W.V. Coscolluels & Associates Architects

Alderwood Mall
Client: The Edward J. DeBartolo Corporation
Structural engineer: Johnson Leifield
Electrical engineer: Nikolakopulos & Associates
Lighting designer: Integrated Lighting Design
Specifications: Ralph P. Mellman & Associates
General contractor: Robert E. Bayley Construction

Al Mamlaka at Kingdom Centre
Client: Kingdom Holding Co.
Al Mamlaka, Retail Center architect: Altoon + Porter Architects LLP
Kingdom Centre architect/engineer: The Consortium of Ellerbe Becket, Inc. and Omrania & Associates
Technical architect/engineer and construction supervisor: Omrania & Associates

Structural engineer: Ove Arup & Partners
Mechanical/electrical engineer: The Building Services Group Ltd.
Quality surveyor: Cotton Thompson & Cole
Safety code: Rolf Jensen & Associates, Inc.
Security: Schiff and Associates
Vertical transportation: Lerch Bates and Associates
General contractor: El Seif Engineering Contracting Establishment

Arden Fair
Client: Homart Development Co.
Structural engineer: Robert Englekirk Structural Engineers, Inc.
Mechanical engineer: Double O Engineering
Electrical engineer: Store Matakovich & Wolfberg
Civil engineer: CH2M Hill
Landscape architect: Lawrence Reed Moline
Public art artists: Joan Brown, Larry Kirkland, Daniel Graffin
Code/fire protection consultant: Rolf Jensen & Associates, Inc.
General contractor: HCB Contractors

The Atrium at Kursky Station

Client: Engeocom

Associate architect: Mosproject–2

Building systems engineering (SMEP): Ove Arup & Partners

Code/fire protection: Ove Arup & Partners

Lighting designer: Joe Kaplan Architectural Lighting

Landscape design: EDAW, Inc.

Signage and graphics: Redmond Schwartz Design, Inc.

Design build contractor: Bouygues

Auchan

Client: Auchan Ipermercati Grouppo Rinascente, sponsored by L'Arca

Botany Town Centre

Client: AMP Henderson Global Investors

Associate architect: Hames Sharley International Ltd.

Project manager: Bovis McLachlan

Structural engineer: Buller George

Service engineer (M/E): Lincolne Scott

Civil engineer: Tonkin & Taylor Ltd.

Acoustic engineer: Kingett Mitchell & Associates Ltd.

Landscape architect: Natural Habitats

Graphic designer: Peter Haythornewaite Design

Public art artist (Kauri Tree): Elizabeth Thompson

Lighting designer: Light Works Ltd.

Traffic design: Traffic Design Group

General contractor: Mainzeal Construction

Chodov Centrum

Client: Rodamco Ceská Republika, Multi Development Corporation nv

Associate architect: Atelier 8000

Structural engineer: Kupros

Building services engineer: Tebodin Czech Republic s.r.o.

Landscape: Delta Vorm, Groep

Geodetic survey: J+F

Traffic: Denis Wilson Partnership, s.r.o.

Denver West

Client: TrizecHahn Centers Management, Inc.

Electrical engineer: Store, Matakovich & Wolfberg

Civil engineer: Paller–Roberts Engineering, Inc.

Environmental graphics: Communication Arts, Inc.

Landscape Architect: Design Workshop

Fashion Show

Client: The Rouse Company

Conceptual design: Richard Orne, AIA, Orne & Associates and Laurin B. Askew, Jr., FAIA, Monk LLC

Design manager for The Rouse Company: Richard Orne, AIA, Orne & Associates

Structural engineers: Ove Arup & Partners; ASI; SME Steel Contractors

Mechanical/plumbing: Tsuchiyama & Kaino

Electrical engineer: Patrick Byrne & Associates

Electrical: B&R Construction Services.

Civil engineer: G.C. Wallace, Inc.

Landscape architect: SWA Group

Code: Rolf Jensen & Associates, Inc.

Cloud canopy: RWDI

Geotechnical engineer: Terracon Consultants Western, Inc.

Geotechnical/environmental: Zipper Zeman Associates, Inc.

Specifications: Chew Specifications

ADA: Stantec Consulting

Acoustics: Paoletti Associates, Inc.

Entertainment systems: Enterscapes Entertainment

Lighting: Kaplan Partner Architectural Lighting; Lightswitch

Parking: Central Parking System; Walker Parking

Traffic engineer: Gorove/Slade Associates, Inc.

Graphics/signage: Sussman/Prejza & Company, Inc.

Audio visual (structural): Vantage Technology Consulting Group

Audio visual consulting: CM Resources, Inc.

Zoning: Mendenhall Moreno and Associates, Inc.

General contractor: The Whiting–Turner Contracting Company

Fashion Valley Center

Client: ERE Yarmouth, Inc.

Structural engineer: Robert Englekirk, Inc.

Electrical engineer: Nikolakopulos & Associates

Plumbing engineer: Store, Matakovich & Wolfberg

Civil engineer: Rick Engineering

Soils engineer: Woodward–Clyde Consultant

Fire protection/building code consultant engineer: Rolf Jensen & Associates, Inc.

Traffic circulation engineer: Linscott, Law & Greenspan Engineer

Traffic engineer: Urban Systems Associates, Inc.

Landscape architect: Wimmer Yamada Associates

Lighting designer: Francis Krahe & Associates

Specifications: Ralph Mellman & Associates

Parking consultant: Walker Parking Consultants/Engineers, Inc.

Cost estimator: Campbell–Anderson & Associates, Inc.

General contractor: Robert E. Bayley Construction

The Gardens on El Paseo

Client: Madison Realty Partnership

Structural engineer: Brandow and Johnston Associates

Mechanical/plumbing engineer: Store, Matakovich & Wolfberg

Electrical engineer: Nikolakopulos & Associates

Civil engineer: ASL Consulting Engineers

Code/fire protection consultant engineers: Rolf Jensen and Associates, Inc.

Landscape architect: Design Workshop

Specifications: Ralph Mellman and Associates

Specialty lighting designer: Patrick Quigley and Associates

Traffic/parking: Linscott, Law & Greenspan

Parking consultant: Walker Parking Consultants

Geology and soils engineers: Earth Systems Consultants

Public art artist (water sculpture): Mineko Grimmer

General contractor: Snyder Landston Real Estate & Services

The Mall at Green Hills

Client: General Growth Center Companies

Structural engineer: Stanley D. Lindsey and Associates, Ltd.

Mechanical engineer: Double O Engineering, Inc.

Electrical engineer: Store Matakovich & Wolfberg

Civil engineer: Barge Waggoner, Sumner and Cannon

Soils engineer: Engineering, Design & Geosciences Group, Inc.

Landscape architect: Roy Ashley & Associates

Building code/fire protection engineer: Rolf Jensen & Associates, Inc.

Parking design: International Parking Design, Inc.

Lighting designer: Wheel Gersztoff Friedman Shankar, Inc.

Construction specifier: Ralph Mellman & Associates

General contractor: McDevitt & Street Co.

GO2 Town

Client: Tai-Tung Development Company (Division of Taiwan Pulp & Paper Corp.)

Associate architect: Fei & Cheng Associates

Traffic: Linscott, Law & Greenspan

Lighting designer: Light Vision Architectural Lighting Design

Graphics designer: Dudrow/Design

Gresham Station

Client: Winmar Company/Trimet

Consulting architect: Zimmer, Gunsul, Frasca Partnership

Structural engineer: KPFF Consulting Engineers

Electrical engineer: Nikolakopulos & Associates

Mechanical engineer: Double O Engineering

Civil engineer: Wilsey & Ham Pacific

Transportation planning: Kittelson & Associates, Inc.

Transit engineer: LTK Engineering Services

EIR consultants: Shapiro & Associates/Eco Northwest

Cost estimating: Sellen Construction Co.

Guangzhou Mega Mall

Client: Goldsun Group

Associate architect: Guangzhou Design Institute

Landscape architect: EDAW EarthAsia Ltd.

Houston Pavilions

Client: Crescent Real Estate Equities, Ltd and Entertainment Development Group

Ka'ahumanu Center

Client: Maui, Land & Pineapple Company, Inc.

Structural engineer: Robert Englekirk, Inc.

Mechanical engineer/subcontractor: Critchfield Mechanical, Inc.

Electrical engineer: Moss Engineering

Civil engineer: Ronald M. Fukumoto Engineering, Inc.

Soils engineer: Dames & Moore

Traffic engineer: Austin, Tsutsumi & Associates, Inc.

Cinema architect consultant: Eugene E. Leucht Architects, Ltd.

Code consultant engineer: Rolf Jensen & Associates, Inc.

Landscape architect: Tongg Clarke & McCelvey Landscape Architects

Lighting designer: Wheel Gersztoff Friedman Shankar, Inc.

Specifications: Ralph Mellman & Associates

Fabric roof: Birdair, Inc.

Construction manager: KX Corporation

General contractor: Keller Construction/ U.S. Pacific Builders, Inc.

Kaleidoscope

Client: Kaleidoscope Partners – Pacific Development Partners & Samsung Pacific Construction Inc.

Structural engineer: ANF & Associates

Mechanical engineer: Store, Matakovich & Wolfberg

Electrical engineer: Nikolakopulos & Associates

Civil engineer: Hall & Foreman, Inc.

Lighting designer: Integrated Lighting Design, Inc.

Code: Rolf Jensen & Associates, Inc.

Parking: RKJK

Soils engineer: Geotechincal Professionals Inc.

Landscape: Stivers & Associates

Specifications: ANC Specification Consultants

Graphics: Maddocks and company

General contractor: Samsung Pacific Construction Inc.

Kirkgate Quarter

Client: Stannifer

Knox City/Towerpoint Centre

Client: AMP Henderson Global Investors

Associate architect: Hames Sharley International Ltd.

Structural/civil engineer: Bonacci Winward

Mechanical/electrical engineer: Simpson Kotzman Pty. Ltd.

Landscape architect: Tract

Fire engineer: ARUP Fire

Specialty lighting: NDY Light

Quantity surveyor: Rawlinsons Pty Ltd.

Traffic: Grogan Richards Pty. Ltd.

Hydraulics: C.J. Arms & Associates

Vertical circulation: Transportation Design Consultants Pty. Ltd.

General contractor: ProBuild

Kowloon Station

Client: Mass Transit Railway Corporation (MTR Corp.)

Associate architect: Leigh & Orange Architects

Associate architect: AGC Design Ltd.

Structural engineer: Ove Arup & Partners

Mechanical/electrical: Parsons Brinckerhoff (Asia) Ltd.

Quantity surveyors: Levett & Bailey Chartered Quantity Surveyors Ltd.

Landscape architect: EDAW EarthAsia Ltd.

Lincolnwood Town Center

Client: Simon Property Group

Associate architect: Christopher Rudolph, AIA

Structural engineer: Tylk, Wright and Gustafson, Inc.

Mechanical engineer: Dolio and Metz, Ltd.

Electrical/plumbing engineer: Technological Engineers, Inc.

Civil engineer: Joseph A. Schudt & Associates

Code consultant engineer: Rolf Jenson Associates, Inc.

Landscape architect: Lawrence Reed Moline, Ltd.

Lighting designer: Theo Kondos, Inc.

General contractor: Inland Construction Co.

Macy*s Department Store Prototype

Client: Federated Department Stores, Inc.

Structural engineer: Nabih Youssef & Associates

M/E/P engineer: Thermaltech Engineering

Civil engineer: Paller–Roberts Engineering, Inc.

Landscape architect: LRM

Cost estimating & specifications: Lonestar Services

Interior: FRCH Design

Code review: Rolf Jensen & Associates

General contractor: Swinerton & Walberg

Marina Square

Client: Marina Centre Holdings Pte. Ltd.

Associate architect: DP Architects Pte. Ltd.

Structural engineer: Meinhardt Pte. Ltd.

Mechanical/electrical engineer: Meinhardt Pte. Ltd. in association with Belmacs Consulting Engineers
Quantity surveyor: Rider Hunt Levett & Bailey
Lighting designer: Light Vision Architectural Lighting Design
Graphics: Dudrow/Design

Market Square at Arden Fair
Client: Morton & Marcy Friedman and Dennis Marks
Structural engineer: Johnson and Nielsen
Mechanical engineer: Paul S. Bennett, Inc.
Civil engineer: CH2M Hill
Electrical/lighting: Nikolakopulos & Associates
Code: Rolf Jensen & Associates
Specifications: Ralph Mellman & Associates
General contractor: Sunseri Construction

The Shops at Mission Viejo
Client: Simon Property Group
Structural engineer: Robert Englekirk, Inc.
M/E/P engineer: S&K Engineers
Civil engineer: EKN Engineering
Lighting designer: Francis Krahe & Associates
Graphics: Redmond Schwartz Design
Fire life safety:
Rolf Jensen & Associates, Inc.
Landscape architect: LRM Ltd.
Specifications: Chew Specification
General contractor: De Bartolo Construction

Mucha Centre
Client: European Property Development
Associate architect: Agiplan
Structural engineer: Ove Arup & Partners
Graphics/signage: Communication Arts Incorporated

Lighting designer: Francis Krahe Associates, Inc.
Hotel designer: Hirsch/Bedner Associates Design

PacifiCenter @ Long Beach
Client: Boeing Realty Corporation
Traffic engineer: Crain & Associates
Civil engineer: Kimley–Horn Associates
Landscape architect: SWA Group

Redmond Town Center
Client: Winmar Company, Inc.
Structural/on-site civil engineer:
KPFF Consulting Engineers
Electrical engineer: Nikolakopulos & Associates
Mechanical engineer: Double O Engineering, Inc.
Code: Rolf Jensen & Associates
Surveyor:
Horton Dennis & Associates, Inc.
Geotechnical: Rittenhouse–Zeman & Associates
Urban design/landscape:
Hewitt–Daly–Isley
Transportation: Entranco Engineers, Inc.
Environmental graphics:
Primo Angeli Inc.
Construction consulting:
Sellen Construction Company, Inc.

Setú Centre
Client: Filo S.A.

Taman Anggrek Mall
Client: PT Mulia IntiPelangi (Mulia Group)
Associate architect: 3 HP
Structural engineer:
Martin, Middlebrook & Louie
Mechanical/electrical engineer:
PCR Engineers Pte Ltd

Code/fire protection: Rolf Jensen & Associates, Inc.
Parking consultant: Kaku Associates
Landscape architect: Emmet L. Wemple & Associates
Lighting designer: Theo Kondos Associates, Inc.
Ice skating rink consultant:
Paul J. Ruffing, AIA
Fountain/water feature:
Aquatic Design Group
Graphic designer: David Carter Design Associates

The Shops at Tanforan
Client: Wattson–Breevast
Structural engineer: Robert Englekirk, Inc.
M/E/P/ engineer: Store, Matakovich & Wolfberg
Civil engineer: Brio Engineering
Fire/life safety: Rolf Jensen & Associates
Soils engineer: Kleinfelder
Landscape architect: LRM Ltd.
Traffic: DKS Associates
Parking: Cary Kopczynski & Co., Inc. P.S.
Graphics:
Redmond Schwartz Mark Design
Lighting designer: Francis Krahe & Associates
Specifications: Chew Specifications
Construction management company:
CM&D
General contractor: The Whiting–Turner Contracting Company

Tower Place
Client: Faison Associates & Noro Realty Advisors
Associate architect (technical):
The FWA Group
Structural engineer: King/Guinn Associates
Mechanical engineer: Benner & Fields
Electrical engineer: Engineers, Inc.

Traffic engineer: Wilbur Smith &
Associates
Life safety/building code engineer:
Rolf Jensen & Associates, Inc.
*Public art artist (salon paintings: 'Winter',
'Spring', 'Summer' & 'Fall'):*
Robert Kushner
Lighting designer: Francis Krahe &
Associates
General contractor: Turner Construction

Triangle Square
Client: Triangle Square Joint Venture
Structural engineer:
KPFF Consulting Engineers
HVAC/plumbing engineer: Double O
Engineering
Electrical engineer: Nikolakopulos &
Associates
Civil: Hall & Foreman, Inc.
Code: Rolf Jensen & Associates
Specifications: Ralph P. Mellman &
Associates
Landscape architect: SWA Group
Parking: International Parking Design
Lighting designer: Wheel Gersztoff
Friedman Associates, Inc.
General contractor: Keller Construction
Co., Inc.

Valencia Town Center Drive
Client: Newhall Land & Farming Co.
and Urban Retail Properties Co.
Structural engineer: Englekirk Partners
M/E/P engineer: Popov Engineers, Inc.
Civil engineer:
Paller–Roberts Engineering, Inc.
Specifications: Chew Specifications
Landscape architect: Kenneth Craig Doyle
Fire code/life safety: Code Consultants
Inc. (CCI)
Lighting designer: Kaplan Partners
Architectural Lighting

Graphics/signage:
Redmond Schwartz Design
Soils engineer: R.T. Frankain &
Associates
General contractor:
Vratsinas Construction Company (VCC)

Victoria Gardens
Client: Forest City Development
California Inc.
Executive architect: KA Inc. Architecture
Design architects: Field Paoli Architects
& Elkus/Manfredi Architects Ltd.
Structural engineer: Thorson Baker and
Associates, Inc.
Mechanical/plumbing engineer: S.Y. Lee
Associates
Electrical engineer: Patrick Byrne &
Associates
Civil engineer: MDS Consulting
Geotechnical engineer: RMA Group
Landscape architect: SWA Group
Lighting designer: Kaplan Partners
Architectural Lighting
Environmental graphics:
Redmond Schwartz Mark Design
Traffic engineer: The Mobility Group
Construction manager:
Vratsinas Construction Company (VCC)
Construction: Forest City Commercial
Construction Co., Inc.

Warringah Mall
Client: AMP Henderson Global
Investors
Associate architect (Phase I):
Thrum Architects Pty Limited
Associate architect (Phase II):
Woods Bagot Pty. Ltd.
Structural engineer: Hyder Consulting
Australia Pty Ltd
Electrical engineer/lighting designer:
Barry Webb & Associates (NSW) Pty Ltd

Code consultant: Scientific Services
Laboratory
Interior design: MBBD
Landscape architect: Site Image
Quantity surveyor: Rider Hunt
Traffic: PPK Environmental &
Infrastructure Pty. Ltd.
Fabric roof: Birdair, Inc.
SpaceTech: Victoria, Australia
Operations: Resolve Engineering
General contractor: Boris Construction

The Waterfront
Client: Vestar Development Company
Civil engineer: Development Resource
Consultants, Inc.
Marine engineer: Moffatt & Nichol
Engineers
Waterfront retail design consultant:
Monk LLC
*Marina waterfront planning/development
consultant:* The Corrough Consulting
Group
Urban design consultant:
Ted Tokio Tanaka Architects